Millennial Myopia
From a Biblical Perspective

BY DR. JENNIFER PATEMAN

Millennial Myopia
From a Biblical Perspective

DR. JENNIFER PATEMAN

BOOK TITLE:
Millennial Myopia, from a Biblical Perspective

WRITTEN BY Dr. JENNIFER PATEMAN
Paperback ISBN: 978-1-909132-67-2
Hardcover ISBN: 978-1-909132-15-3
eBook ISBN: 978-1-909132-68-9

Published By:
APMI Publications
In Partnership with Truth for the Journey Books **2**
Email: publications@alanpateman.com
www.AlanPatemanMinistries.com

Acknowledgements:
Author: Dr. Jennifer Pateman
Computer Administration/Office Manager: Dr. Dorothea Struhlik
Cover Design: Dr.P.
Cover Image Credit: © alanpateman

❖

Dedication

Jesus is my Alpha and Omega. My husband has also been a rock in my life as my God-given mentor and best friend. I tell him everyday, "You are my favourite person in the whole world!" He's a wonderful man of God, loving husband, father and the love of my life. Alan, I thank God, for all that is *you*.

To my three extremely bright children, Andrew James, Naomi and Abigail, I love you more than words can say. You and Dad are the best thing that ever happened to me. My blessings truly overflow.

❖

To All Generations...

"For the Lord is good; his mercy is everlasting; and his truth endureth **to all generations.**"

(Psalm 100:5 KJVS)

❖

Table of Contents

❖

Foreword

One morning I was watching a certain cable news channel, with my morning coffee when I saw a random interview, with a young 19-year-old called Patrick Finnegan. It's captioned title online was: **"Teenage venture capitalist Patrick Finnegan has a message for corporate America: Look out for Gen Z."**

Watching this interview introduced me to a new concept. Not only was I just getting to grips with the concept of Millennials (used *ad-nauseam* by the media); I now had to embrace another new buzzword. A new cohort, hot on the heels, ready to out-mode, out-smart and even out-brand, these Millennials. What an enigma! Who can stop such savvy progress and whatever will come next?

A little bemused, yet engaged, I continued to listen as Mr Finnegan described himself as an "influencer" and a "disruptor." Saying, **"I'm going to be a mogul. I want to disrupt the [establishment] because it needs to be disrupted."**

Once finished I went and did a little research of my own. I wanted to know if this kid was just pushing a new and trendy narrative to enrich himself or whether there really was something to this? I wanted to have the specifics on each demographic and to find out who they were. How old they were. How different their thinking was and why they thought that way.

I'm not talking psychoanalysis; rather I wanted to see where God was in all of this and how to navigate. So I began with the Millennials, only to find that few things are truly unique to them. The lines blur and so in their defence, at the very onset, I want to say that human nature (specifically the fallen nature) is the major common denominator. Notwithstanding, *some* things are unique to the Millennials, so let's take a look.

❖

Introduction

This book is a compilation of research, mostly on the subject of demographics from a biblical perspective. It was written while researching for a dissertation and has been adapted into a book.

Demography is a global subject; therefore the various social studies and research that has been compiled for this book, along with the many authors who have been quoted, represent several different countries around the world, mostly the UK, Europe and America.

The title, **"Millennial Myopia"** refers to the *short sightedness* that exists within the world today, surrounding Millennials. We are led to believe, especially by the media, that if we don't fit into a particular box, we must be irrelevant. But not so fast!

For example, it's my firm belief that God is not finished with the Baby Boomer Generation. Take our family: my husband is a Baby Boomer, I am Generation X and our children comprise both Millennials and Gen Z (it will all make sense!)

So I am rather happy to champion each demographic cohort because I've had the personal pleasure and experience of witnessing how each generation has something rich to offer.

From the youngest to the oldest, Gen Zers might be demanding and exciting but the Baby Boomers have a wealth of life experience and most of them are not ready to be put out to graze just yet. They still have a weighty contribution to make.

"When you cease to make a contribution, you begin to die."

– Eleanor Roosevelt

For instance, at the time of writing this book, Baby Boomer Donald Trump, (who relatively recently has only just embarked on his political career), managed to bag the White House! His becoming President has changed the political paradigm forever. Things will never be done the same. Along with his unconventional no-nonsense style, he happily dominates the *Twitterverse* like we've never seen any other political figure do before. He's simply a force of nature. With energy levels that make men half his age keel over! So, quite clearly, Baby Boomers aren't to be messed with and they're still in the game.

14

For those who are much younger, studies reveal that while Millennials might on average use three screens, Gen Zers use five: a smartphone, TV, laptop, desktop, and iPad and possess an attention span of approximately eight seconds, (which describes just about everyone I know!)

I think we've all had to adapt somehow and while our children might be far more adept on social media, we are by no means dinosaurs!

So how does any of this impact the church? It strengthens it. Why? Because what the church is said to be losing in numbers, it's gaining in strength. Meaning that the squishy middle is being dealt with and the ones left standing are more serious about their faith. The contrasts are sharper, everywhere, from the political Left to the political Right, and everything in-between, which includes the church.

More people are making a stand for what they believe, one way or another. So basically it's considered a win-win for the church; eliminating the fuzzy grey areas is just what She needs.

While demography is a secular pursuit, that aids business marketing and media branding, it's still influencing the church nonetheless.

So as we look at the nuts and bolts of this peculiar subject, I hope you enjoy the read, as much as I enjoyed the research.

Stay blessed.
Doctor Jennifer Pateman

❖

CHAPTER 1

Understanding the Millennials

P rior to this research, it was already obvious to me, that many in our churches have adopted or been influenced by this so-called "Millennial-mind-set." It's nothing new. For example it's nothing new for folks to expect *participation-trophies* just for showing up. Or having commitment and entitlement issues; demanding a *reward-based-gospel,* while never being required to unpack their suitcases (spiritually speaking). People have always had these kinds of fleshly issues. Perhaps it's a lot more pronounced these days and just needed branding with a new label.

Furthermore, we can't be led to believe that Millennials are the only ones with *commitment fatigue,* because things like church-surfing or church-hopping have always existed.

Many have failed to stay planted where God put them, so that He could mould, shape and train them to serve as true disciples.

Yet commitment fatigue is a huge issue for Millennials who on the surface of things, appear to be very committed, because of their tendency to be very "cause-orientated." They always need a "cause" to fight for or protest against. But in reality, the research reveals that for many Millennials, *true* commitment, even on the smallest level, represents a real cramp.

Some would say it's their need for autonomy, others would say it's just youthful rebellion. Or perhaps it's their short attention span or something more deep-seated within their culture.

However, according to young Millennial writer Kirsten Mikesell, who is arguably an expert on her own generation: "Many Millennials can barely make it through a song without skipping to the next one, let alone make it through a book before picking up another. We can open and close tabs on a computer faster than our grandparents can blink, and don't even ask us how many apps we currently have open."

Haven't we all yielded to the information age in some way and become overloaded and bloated? Educated beyond our level of willingness or obedience, opinionated beyond our level of commitment?

Apparently when adopting a Millennial mind-set, it's all about freedom. One must view *affiliation* as unnecessary and the need for *de-tanglement* as a prime element of survival! **Shallow is good because the more meaningless the attachments are in our lives, the less risk it poses to our individuality.**

Mikesell insists that for her generation this is the **Golden Age of Disaffiliation:** "We are generally unattached to politics and religion. As a matter of fact, the Pew Research Center says 50% of Millennials identify as political independents, and 29% say they're not affiliated with any religion. But… it's not like we dislike being a part of groups and events. Just take social networking, for example. **I'll take affiliation with Facebook, Instagram, and Twitter any day!**"

When it comes to life's *ultimate* commitment, she admits: "We're choosing the single life over marriage…" not because we're, "entirely against marriage, but we don't like to settle down. **We're opportunists, we believe in** *carpe diem,* **and we believe in love, but not at the expense of giving up our lifestyles.**"[1]

Once again, people in every age bracket have identified with such narcissistic philosophies and ideas; nothing's truly unique. **In fact every generation develops its own brand of selfishness and thinks it holds exclusive rights on self-preservation!**

The Subculture of Slacktivism

This leads me, ever so briefly, to something called "slacktivism." Basically this unwillingness to commit to anything meaningful is not limited to one group or another.

And with the likes of Twitter, Facebook and Instagram, "slacktivism" has been bred on the notion that participation in random online-petitions actually changes the world.

The Urban Dictionary declares that a slacktavist is one "...who vigorously posts political propaganda and petitions in an effort to affect change in the world without leaving the comfort of the computer screen!"

Delusion at best, "slacktivism," is a play-on-words between, "slacker" and "activism." The idea is, that you get to play both judge and jury - of human events - while sitting on the comfort and anonymity of your own sofa. **Having zero accountability or responsibility, slacktivism is considered so safe, even a coward could do it!**

In fact few people today are held accountable for their online views. Cyber bullying is the result. From their secret bubble, they can spew visceral hatred and slander that ultimately ruins lives, without ever being answerable.

Bleeding into the Stereotype

Again, the point I'm alluding to is this, that there are many sides to this culture that we live in and the generations that we were born into. Things are more common than we are led to believe. It's not confined to one age bracket. People who go online - of all age groups - are engaging in slacktivism. But this is just one example.

As you continue to read, you will discover that certain characteristics, such as "multi-tasking," are not unique to Millennials either, (18-34 year olds).

For example, even though my husband is a Baby Boomer, there are days when I see him multi-task to such a degree that he defies his own generation. For instance, he can be working at his computer writing, doing emails, updating his Facebook page and simultaneously be responding to international text messages and talking to someone on the telephone. Sometimes in addition to this, there's either breaking news on the TV in the background, worship music playing or preaching on YouTube.

In fact, our home feels more like a *nerve-centre* than a home, at times! It's a think-tank and HQ. It's an active place.

My husband would never have been so flexible, without adapting to his environment. Where utilizing such resources of technology and information, is just common sense.

As a high achiever my husband's attitude is this: **"If I can go around the globe three times in one day without leaving my desk - making my life easier, more productive, less costly and less exhausting – then it's a no-brainer!"**

Of course he does leave his desk, but my point is that if you're an achiever, you're going to find ways to achieve no matter what your age or situation. Time-economy is a big issue for all of us, whether for young mothers or business executives, we all need more time and want to save as much of it as possible, without wasting any of it. Anything too expensive on our time must be adjusted quickly to avoid stress.

"As you get older it's imperative to pace yourself," my husband adds, "because it's counterproductive to fight the aging process. Instead you must recognise the season you're in, adjust to it and continue being productive. You can achieve the same results, with less expenditure, if you're smart about it."

So once again, as we discuss Millennials, I am aware that all lines get crossed and blurred. We are all capable of bleeding into the demographic stereotype, no matter what our age. But let's proceed to understand the landscape that we are all now a part of and try to see how it applies to us and how we can utilize it for God's kingdom.

After all, as believers we are not part of some corporate machine, that's trying to manipulate the masses. We are agents of love, looking to get the good news of Jesus Christ to a dying but ever changing world.

❖

CHAPTER 2

Generation Y (Millennials)

The scope of my research doesn't just encompass one single generation but several, from the Baby Boomers to Generation Z.

It does seem comical to me now that we refer to generations this way, nonetheless there is gravity to it, simply because generational gaps do exist. They mark generational shifts, whether advancements in science and technology or other fields, revealing surges in development that help brand each generation with their own distinctive mark.

However, as we are talking about Millennials, first I must point out that depending on whom you talk to and where you get your information from, some researchers say that Generation Y doesn't technically exist.

Such as French researcher, Prof. Jean Pralong who debunks the Millennial Generation by saying, "For economists, a generation is constituted of people who confront the same conditions at work. The study showed that no difference exists between 25-year-olds and 45-year-olds at work. **This shows that on a scientific level, Generation Y doesn't exist."**

Prof. Pralong also added, "The concept of Generation Y was invented so that managers between 35 to 45 years old could blame the younger generation for their fear of changes in the workplace – especially technological changes. Members of Generation X are subjected to constant and growing pressure at work. They are worried and unmotivated, but given their stature, it's not easy to admit. So they find a scapegoat."

Natalie Kettne of RHevista said that, "Pralong undertook the study because he realized that most perceptions of Generation Y were based on anecdotes told by managers or recommendations by consultants. **The large majority of what has been written about Generation Y has not been based on official studies."**[1]

Consequently, a look at Millennials wouldn't be complete without first acknowledging the fact that there are some real Millennial *deniers* out there. Who, for many differing reasons assert that Generation Y doesn't really exist. Nevertheless they are here amongst us, alive and well. And we can't seem to hear enough about this particular generation, that shouldn't really exist. And whether "invented" by big business and the media or not, Millennials it seems, are here to stay.

So call it evolution if you like but each generation does have different influential factors or "influencers" and "disrupters," as young Mr Finnegan likes to call them. We need to know how each demographic ticks, in order to reach them in their orbit. In other words, we have to meet them where they are, not where we perceive that they should be.

So to pursue my original premise, these vital questions should be asked of any generation: who, what, where, why and how? Who identifies as a Millennial, what are their beliefs and ideas, where is their purpose and legacy felt most and how will it impact the culture, Christianity and the church?

Relevance v. Authenticity

We must ask such questions because if we are too antiquated or out-of-touch to bother, then our influence on the younger generations will be lost. This doesn't mean that we must *be-relevant-at-all-costs*. No! Yet we owe it to them, to instruct them. **Remembering that the good news of the gospel can *seamlessly* transition any and all generations, because its saving truth is *always* relevant.**

My research confirmed to me that younger demographics are not looking for older generations to be "relevant" so much as "authentic." **Authenticity is more important to them, than relevancy or anything else.** The church then must not strive to be relevant at the cost of authenticity. That's exactly what they're looking for. In fact it is estimated that Millennials in massive numbers are turning to Christ for this very reason. **There is no one more authentic than Jesus.**

So while most secular Millennials struggle with commitment fatigue, the opposite can be true of those who turn to Christ. In great numbers Millennials are turning to God and are *all-in* about their faith, creating global excitement. Hillsongs and many other churches and organizations are catering for the Millennial believer.

All said and done, we do live in a world that now favours all things Millennial. This can be both positive and negative. Firstly let me say that I am pro-Millennial myself, as I have Millennial children. Nonetheless we can't fall into the trap of narrowing everything down or limiting our scope and our message to reach just one specific demographic, at the exclusion of all others. I see this as dangerous and misguided, (hence the title for this book, which is better explained in the next chapter).

One obvious example of this would be to ostracise certain age groups, who don't fit in. Such as having church groups where anyone over the age of 30 are no longer welcome, (some family friends of ours had first hand experience of this in London). Again, this is a trap that the corporate world has fallen into and must be avoided by the church.

I hasten to add however, that it's not always the Millennials themselves who are making such mistakes; rather it's those who are blindly trying to cater for them, with ulterior motives.

Maturity v. Immaturity

Here is a brief culture reference concerning a popular British band from the 1960's called "The Who." In 1965

Roger Daltrey, lead vocalist, famously claimed that he would kill himself before reaching 30 because he didn't want to get old. Later in life however, the explanation given about such lyrics as, **"...hope I die before I get old,"** was that this was a reference to *attitude* and not to physical age.

Incidentally the song in question was titled, "My Generation," which reinforces the point that each generation feels qualified to set its own limitations. Yes ageism has always been alive and well but as my level-headed 21 year old son said to me recently, "Why should we allow big business or big media to label *any* of us? Whatever happened to just calling young people, 'young'?" (Warning: young people know it, even when the media is patronizing them).

Next, appealing to an even younger audience was the animation film that came out in 2005 when my children were much younger, called "Robots." A film that was all about being *upgraded* with the catch phrase that went something like this: **"Why be you, when you can be new!"** The underlying message was that everybody has a sell-by-date. A threshold where your life becomes obsolete and must be replaced with a newer shinier model.

A bogus trajectory, considering Mozart and Beethoven whose masterpieces are well over 100 years old and still perfect! Proof that not *everything* needs upgrading.

Generally speaking though, *maturity* isn't celebrated by the wider culture, especially the entertainment industry. So it's little wonder when our younger generations find themselves socially challenged if they openly respect or show value for it, in any way. Which of course is driven by a strong liberal media but not by scripture.

For instance one could interpret Malachi 4:6 as God's warning against generational divisions, where a separation between maturity and immaturity exists. God calls for them to reunite: "He shall turn the heart of the fathers to the children, and the heart of the children to their fathers, lest I come and smite the earth with a curse."

We will look at this scripture again, later on in this book, but it is suffice to say, the context is no less fitting for today. The enemy of mankind has always understood the consequences of division, thus his wild promotion of it on every platform and in every context: division in government, in the family, the workplace, and in marriage, between the sexes and so forth.

Perhaps the most damaging, is the division between maturity and immaturity, the seasoned veterans versus the rookies. **When the baton is dropped, the race is forfeited and so is the next generation.**

❖

CHAPTER 3

The Harvest
is Gathered at Maturity

Perché è la terra che da sola fa crescere il raccolto. Dapprincipio spunta una foglia, poi si forma la spiga e finalmente il grano. **E quando il grano è <u>maturo,</u> il contadino viene subito** con la falce per mieterlo (Marco 4:28-29 La Bibbia della Gioia).

*The earth produces crops by itself; first the blade, then the head [of grain], then the **mature** grain in the head. But when the crop **ripens**, he **immediately** puts in the sickle [to reap], because [the time for] the harvest has come.*
(Mark 4:28-29 AMP)

For those who don't know, the Italian word for "ripe" is "maturo," as seen above. Which is remarkably close to the

English word mature, which also means: *ripe, fully developed, established, complete and so forth.* Notice too, that as soon as the farmer recognizes the ripeness and maturity of his crop, he moves in for the harvest, *"immediately,"* ("il contadino viene subito").

The Feast of Tabernacles Celebrated Maturity

I don't want to labour on this point, but one good example of God's attitude towards maturity is The Feast of Tabernacles, which showcases His desire for us to celebrate the time of harvest, which in turn represents maturity. There is so much revelation that can be gathered from studying this particular festival but I will stay on topic, (otherwise this book will never end!)

To be clear, no harvest is gathered before its full quota of time. In other words, before it's ripe and ready. And although the Hebrew word Sukkot means: Feast of Booths, (or Tabernacles as it is better known in the English), it is also known as: "Feast of the Ingathering."

The double meaning for Sukkot was both *historical* and *agricultural.* Historically Sukkot represents the forty-year period during which the children of Israel wandered in the desert and dwelt in temporary shelters or "booths." Secondly, from an agricultural standpoint, Sukkot is seen as a harvest festival, celebrating the end of year "ingathering" or the final gathering of the harvest.

As it says in The Voice translation of the bible below, it was during The Feast of Tabernacles that the Israelites were to make temporary shelters and live in them for a week to remember how they lived in temporary shelters when they left Egypt.

This festival is considered the longest and most joyful of the Jewish festivals, a celebration that lasted seven straight days! **Proof that God really wants us to share His joy in the harvest, a symbol of maturity and provision:**

> *Celebrate with your sons and daughters, your male and female slaves, and the Levites, foreigners, orphans, and widows who live in your city.* ***Celebrate for seven days*** *in honor of the Eternal your God, in the place the Eternal will choose. The Eternal your God will bless you with abundant produce;* ***He will bless everything you do, and you'll have a lot to celebrate!***
>
> *Three times each year, every male* ***Israelite*** *must appear before Him in the place He chooses for the Feast of Unleavened Bread* ***(Passover),*** *for the Feast of Weeks* ***(Pentecost),*** *and for* ***the Feast of Shelters (Tabernacles).*** *Don't come empty-handed! Decide what amount you want to contribute* ***voluntarily*** *out of what He has blessed you with, and bring that as a gift.*
> (Deuteronomy 16:13-17 VOICE)

True maturity is not celebrated enough today, only in rare circles. Yet the Feast of Tabernacles reveals to us that after collecting the ripe harvest, we are to have the biggest party of all, to rejoice and commemorate the fruit of investment: increase, multiplication, maturity, ripeness, readiness, development, establishment and completion.

In human terms, investment represents cost. It's expensive being invested in something and is best described as having some "skin in the game." For example, there's a great deal of investment that goes into a harvest: toil, sweat, along with much time and patience. But when the fullness of time arrives God wants us to celebrate it, *big time* but not *before* time.

> *He has made everything beautiful and appropriate in its time.*
>
> (Ecclesiastes 3:11 AMP)

Not Swayed by the Culture

There is a time for everything. For example, who ever held a pre-harvest-festival or a pre-graduation-ceremony?

Harvest time celebrates achievement and human character as much as history or agriculture. Where lifetime achievements are recognized and celebrated including the harvest of souls that produces a celebration in heaven.

People even celebrate retirement, when they reach a ripe old age! **"You will arrive hearty *and undiminished* at the grave after a long life, like a pile of grain harvested at its peak ripeness"** (Job 5:26 VOICE).

So although we see that it's countercultural to celebrate maturity today, we must do it anyway! We must celebrate God's increase in our lives, as Paul said it best: "I have planted, Apollos watered; **but God gave the increase,"** (1 Corinthians 3:6). Only God can bring us to a place of personal maturity and fulfillment, only God can mature the human heart.

We must share His joy and not be swayed by the culture. As Proverbs 10:22 says, "The blessing of the Lord brings [true] riches, and **He adds no sorrow** to it [for it comes as a blessing from God]" (AMP).

We are meant to experience increase, in every area of our lives. God sanctions true progress. "We know [with great confidence] that God [who is deeply concerned about us] causes all things to work together [as a plan] for good for those who love God, to those who are called according to His plan *and* purpose" (Romans 8:28 AMP).

It's always God's purpose that we experience personal development, growth and maturity; it just requires *time-investment*.

Farmers understand the law of "seed-*time*-and-harvest" and that harvest is gathered at maturity not before. But they also understand that while it may take just one day to sow the seed into the ground, it takes *many* days to collect the harvest, because the seed has multiplied.

Therefore maturity and increase bring a greater workload and responsibility. So we better be ready! And although this book focuses mostly on Millennials and Gen Zers, I would urge that maturity never be abandoned because immaturity can't always handle the responsibility.

"The price of greatness is responsibility."
- Winston Churchill

Delayed Gratification is now Old School

The current culture laments the *cost* of maturity. The concept of waiting for *anything* is old school. In fact any form of *delayed gratification* is old school (discipline, restraint or self control). **If you can have it now, why wait?**

Waiting is always going to be a labour of love, but maturity is worth the while. As we saw in biblical culture, maturity brings joy, celebration and feasting, but in the same token immaturity was *never* celebrated. (Even the birth of Jesus represented the fullness of time where prophecy was concerned).

Lastly, remember how Jesus responded to the unyielding fig tree, which should have been ready with ripe figs for Him to eat for breakfast? Apart from using it symbolically as an object lesson for His disciples, Jesus clearly didn't celebrate *fruitlessness* (see Matthew 21:18-22).

Just like the fig tree, everything about our lives or generation can seem in place, but when you get up close, is it *sterile* or *unavailable* for Jesus? It's critical that we realise how badly the next generation needs our instruction, to help bring them to a place of maturity. Any division propagated between successive generations, only sets them up for a fall.

Besides God will hold us partly responsible if the next generation is ill prepared and found wanting when He comes, **"You have been weighed on the scales and found wanting"** (Daniel 5:27 NIV).

❖

CHAPTER 4

Millennial Myopia is a Trap

So there are consequences to generational divides and yet modern culture continually promotes such divisions. The word *"myopia"* is a medical term that opticians use for *short sightedness*. But it can also describe an attitude that is out of focus. **Millennial myopia refers to a blind fixation that the media and even the church have adopted towards Generation Y.**

In every sphere of thinking, extreme views exist. For Millennials it's no different. Some consider Millennials as non-existent (scientifically speaking) while others see them as an all-consuming factor. **In other words, either they're the best generation that ever walked the earth or the worst!**

Here is an article that describes what it is to be *socially myopic* from a corporate perspective, which champions the

Millennial Generation above and beyond, (at the expense of) every other generation.

The article is entitled: "Millennial Myopia: A Big Social Media Trap," and it says the following,

"Mitigating Millennial Myopia: Social Media Beyond Gen Y. The problem with the oversimplification of **'social media is for the young' is that it implicitly discredits social media as a platform for reaching everyone else.** A report comes out that Millennials are quitting Facebook, and the marketing world immediately begins looking for other places to direct their efforts. This is a dangerous and faulty knee-jerk reaction. **Hundreds of millions of other potential customers are still there, and with less cynicism and overexposure, are probably more receptive to your messages anyway.**

In my opinion, the blanket efficacy of social media for Millennial marketing is yet another misconception. Companies often believe that just because they use social media personally, Millennials will automatically be its best — or worse, only — targets from a business perspective. I have spoken with countless financial advisors who use social media for business and have had **better success reaching new clients of all ages — particularly those in the 35-to-55 age bracket.**

A recent example of social media Millennial myopia comes from BNY Mellon and the University of

Oxford's Said Business School. In "Want to Win Millennials? Don't Bet on Social Media," they concluded that less than 1% of Millennials want financial services providers to connect with them through social media. **The implication of the article is that if Millennials aren't biting on social media, no one will. This assumption, again, is incorrect."**[1]

Ahead of the Curve with Jesus

So although the article above is speaking from a corporate perspective, in my mind it's a relevant warning to the church. The short sightedness and narrow mindedness of the corporate world had them going after the Millennials so hard, that they managed to discredit (even show intolerance towards) all other cohorts in the process. Not clever! It's a mistake that has cost them dearly and not something that the church needs to emulate.

So since largely miscalculating the Millennials, the corporate world doesn't want to make the same mistake when it comes to Gen Z. So they are feverishly studying them, to get ahead of the curve. And as this pace quickens, where will the church find itself in the coming decades?

Spiritual Myopia

Firstly we must recognise myopia within the church (spiritually speaking) and not get mired in the same quicksand. If we are going to recognise demographics at all, then we must recognise all of them as being important, not just the most recent.

Nor are we contending with the business world for these Millennials, because our motivation for reaching them is love not greed, which are vastly different. And while the business and political worlds collide, as they try and solicit the buying and voting powers of this particular cohort, the church's job is diametrically different. It's her responsibility to get something *"to"* Millennials and not *"from"* them, such as instruction, guidance and truth. But how is she going to achieve this?

While everyone else is striving to get ahead of the curve, the church should already be there. The saving message of Jesus Christ is unstoppable. Considering that everything Jesus did while on earth was not only redemptive but also counter-cultural. He spoke to Samaritans; He talked to women, forgave sins, turned tables and healed on the Sabbath and so on. Jesus was and still is the ultimate "disrupter" of the religious and political establishment, status quo and corruption.

In this context, where truth *offends,* Jesus is exhibit-A, "We preach Christ crucified: a stumbling block... and foolishness" (1 Corinthians 1:22-24).

Politically correct elitism and stagnant status quo have always hated Jesus, along with the religious order and hierarchy. He is their stumbling block whose truth still offends today. In the previous chapter I spoke about relevance versus authenticity. **Well, Jesus is the ultimate** *authenticity* **that everyone's looking for; they just haven't realized it yet!**

❖

CHAPTER 5

Your Time
Runs out with Logan's Run

At its extreme, social myopia is a dangerous game of manipulation, which narrows the collective focus onto one chosen group, while simultaneously devaluing all else. We see this for example when the mainstream media exhibits bias for a favoured candidate in an election campaign, such as democrats versus republicans for example or liberals versus conservatives. Hitler's ambition for an "Aryan race" is just one example of extreme social myopia.

In reference to this my husband reminded me of a film from many years ago called "Logan's Run." Many will remember it. In 1967 this science fiction novel was written by William F. Nolan and George C. Johnson and was later adapted into its film version in 1976.

Is the Modern Church becoming Ageist?

The original novel depicted a, *"dystopic* ageist future society in which both population and the consumption of resources are maintained in equilibrium by requiring the death of everyone reaching the age of 21."[1]

Although the book is slightly more extreme than the film, the context is the same, once you reach a certain age you were *obsolete*.

"In the world of 2116, a person's maximum age is strictly legislated: twenty-one years, to the day. When people reach this *lastday* they report to a *sleepshop* in which they are willingly executed via a pleasure-inducing toxic gas. A person's age is revealed by their *palm flower* (called *life clock* in the film) crystal embedded in the palm of their right hand that **changes colour every seven years, yellow (age 0-6), then blue (age 7-13), then red (age 14-20), then blinks red and black on lastday, and finally turns black at 21...**

The film only uses the basic premise from the novel (everyone must die at a specific age...) However, the world is post apocalyptic and people now live inside a huge domed city and are unaware of the world outside, believing it to be a barren, poisonous environment. The motivations of the characters are also quite different in the film. **The age of death is 30,**

and instead of reporting to a sleepshop, citizens must take part in a ritual called 'carrousel' in which they are vaporized with the chance of being 'renewed.'"[2]

Denying the Process

Notice the use of different colours to differentiate between the generations? Today we use complicated demography instead!

The main point is that ageism and segregation, which systematically separates maturity from immaturity (the fathers from the sons), is also influencing the church. The denial of due process - maturation and ripening - is the denial of God who created it. Scripture says that God nurtures and trains every child that He loves, which is of itself a process.

Even Jesus did not skip the human maturation process. (Our youngest daughter called Jesus, "God with skin on!") Yes He was born in the flesh, but Jesus was not born in his early thirties! He went through a process like the rest of us, learning obedience and arriving at "the full stature of maturity."

Though he was God's Son, he learned trusting-obedience by what he suffered, just as we do ... having arrived at the full stature of his maturity.
(Hebrews 5:8-10 MSG)

The Lord disciplines those He loves, and He corrects each one He takes as His own.
(Hebrews 12:6 VOICE)

41

*The Eternal proves His love by **caring enough** to discipline
you, just as a father does his child, his **pride and** joy.*
(Proverbs 3:12 VOICE)

Progress Passes the Baton

**Without each successive generation passing on what
they've learnt to the next, we'd still be in the dark ages!**
There'd be zero progress. The only reason technology and
science have advanced, is because each generation has had
an obligation to pass that knowledge along. The church is no
different. Revelation is progressive and is passed on to the
next generation.

Maturity is gained through many trials and tribulations.
The lessons of which can't be lost on our younger
generations. We owe it to them to instruct them and they
owe it to themselves to be teachable. Certain pitfalls have
been avoided by studying church history. Bestsellers such as
the, "God's Generals" series by Roberts Liardon for example
have helped many to appreciate the prophetic passing-of-
the-baton.

**Since time and maturity go hand in hand, more often
than not we grow weary of the process.** Yet maturity must
never be discarded or discredited because of our own
impatience. Just like the most valued wines and cheeses, it
can take considerable time to bring something (or someone)
to maturity. Only then can they offer the fullest flavours. On
the other hand, if maturity or the *fullness of time* is disregarded,
it's of detriment to us all – we are all robbed.

When the fullness of the time was come, God sent forth his Son, *made of a woman, made under the law, to redeem them that were under the law, that we might receive the adoption of sons.*

(Galatians 4:4-5 KJV)

Precept must be upon precept, precept upon precept; line upon line, line upon line; here a little, and there a little...

(Isaiah 28:10 KJV)

❖

CHAPTER 6

Generational Separation Ushers in Total Destruction

I will send the prophet Elijah to you before that great and dreadful day of the Lord comes. **He will turn the hearts of the parents to their children, and the hearts of the children to their parents; OR ELSE I WILL COME AND STRIKE THE LAND WITH <u>TOTAL DESTRUCTION</u>** (Malachi 4:5-6 NIV emphasis added).

Malachi above concerns generational detachment and this is a subject very close to my husband's heart. Here's a segment from one of his Facebook posts from a while back:

"I want to humbly confront all Millennial-minded people not to divorce themselves from their spiritual parents (Ephesians 6:1/Malachi 4:6). It's time for spiritual wayward sons to honour their fathers and for fathers to honour their sons by changing their ways and assuming the role that God intended them to have. To take spiritual responsibility in raising up and releasing spiritual sons (this includes daughters). This requires a turning of both parties, fathers turning to their children and children turning to their fathers" (Alan Pateman 2016).

Malachi 4:5-6 above is explicit and unambiguous; if there is a generational divide the result is **"total destruction."** It's a warning to every generation. Why? We are designed to rely on each other, to work together and advance each other. The previous generation has an all-out-obligation to instruct the newer, especially in the things of God, **particularly His Word.** Every bloodline must continue in the knowledge of God. "If a house is divided against itself, that house cannot stand" (Mark 3:25 NIV). **When that vital connection between the generations is lost or destroyed, it's a win-win for the enemy.**

Christ's Non-Myopic Commission

The Commission Christ gave us is 100% non-myopic. It's non-parochial because it's all-encompassing and all-inclusive. I say this in the context that God desires NONE should perish. So going into "all the world" requires strategy that embraces "all the world." But what exactly does "all the world" look like? Some will say that generation gaps don't exist in the kingdom of God and therefore demographics are irrelevant.

Yet the fact of the matter is that generation gaps *do* exist and heavily influence people living in "all the world." So there's no escaping it. And if the corporate world are willing to study these cohorts just to brand and market them for their money, how much more should we be willing to identify them, so we can reach them for the kingdom of God?

Each generation is marked by its own advancements, in areas such as knowledge and technology, which have had profound influence. If for example you take my formative years (where the Internet was non-existent) versus my children's formative years, which have never known life *without* the Internet or smart gadgets – the impact on individual development has been significantly different.

Our youngest daughter in particular has never known life without an iPad or smart phone. In some homes it's the Internet that's raising children or at least providing a cheap babysitter!

Younger Generations Require Instruction

I was listening to Pat Robertson on the 700 Club one morning over breakfast, talking about the younger generation's need for *instruction,* which reinforces the point yet again. Now consider this passage in Isaiah and the controversial issue that it raises.

> *Oh, **how I ache for** my people! They are **oppressed by children, ruled by women, <u>naïve and inexperienced</u>.** O my people, your leaders are misleading you, guiding you down the path to disaster.*
>
> *(Isaiah 3:12 VOICE)*

47

In this culture of political correctness that we find ourselves today, this would be considered offensive for being either sexist or ageist. Yet it's neither. Rather I would suggest to you that in context with the time it was written, both women and children were the weakest, most vulnerable and most uneducated members of their society. Therefore the implication would be, that it's disastrous to be led by those who are **"naïve and inexperienced."** They lack instruction and wisdom and as the King James Version says, such people, "...cause thee to err."

Perhaps more scathing is the Living Bible's rendition of this particular verse: "O my people! Can't you see what fools your rulers are? Weak as women! Foolish as little children playing king. True leaders? No, misleaders! Leading you down the garden path to destruction" (Isaiah 3:12 TLB).

This brings to mind the young unopposed leader of North Korea's "Supreme People's Assembly," Kim Jong-un. Conflicting sources say that he's approximately between 32 and 34 years old, which also makes him a Millennial - no less!

In addition, Kim was listed as, the World's 46th most powerful person, by Forbes in 2013. Perhaps he should have made it onto the world's most dangerous list too! **Point being, that without quality instruction, the next generation will always be misguided and dangerous.**

❖

CHAPTER 7

The Generation Gap Defined

What is the generation gap and why is it relevant? According to the Work and Family Researchers Network, the generation gap is defined as follows: "The differences in values, lifestyles, and economic opportunities that exist between people of different age cohorts living in the same society."[1]

According to one dictionary definition, the generation gap is defined as, **"the vast differences in terms of attitudes, experiences and taste between people born a certain amount of time apart who are living at the same time.** An example of a generation gap is the knowledge of the older Baby Boomers about computers versus the knowledge of young people born after the Internet had already exploded and taken off."[2]

The key emphasis here is that besides all the differences between the cohorts, right now we're still all living at the *same point in history* and inhabiting the same planet. Therefore regardless of our differences we *must* cohabit. We must appreciate the differences and move on *together* because "different" is good not bad.

Let's say just for example that my husband and I had raised ten children instead of three, and that they all lived in the *same* house, had the *same* parents, ate the *same* food, drank the *same* water, read the *same* books, went to the *same* church, even to the *same* school, had the *same* friends, opportunities and prospects. I can tell you now, that they would all be *different*. Their individuality would be guaranteed no matter how much they shared in common.

We must never stifle individuality. There aren't two fingerprints the same and for good reason. Therefore being *diverse* is healthy and good, whether at home or away.

"Remember always that you not only have the right to be an individual, you have an obligation to be one."

– Eleanor Roosevelt

Demographic Cohort Overview

Not everyone understands the jargon about demographics that's being brandished around today. The following is a helpful breakdown, using familiar names and faces to help us identify each cohort through a modern lens.

Baby Boomers

"The Baby Boomers are a generation of people born during the post WWII 'baby boom', roughly during the years 1946 to 1964. In the years following WWII many western nations experienced a spike in births as they slowly recovered from the economic hardships experienced during wartime.

This new generation of Baby Boomers experienced an unprecedented level of economic growth and prosperity throughout their lifetime. They entered the world in a time of relative hardship, but thanks to education, government subsidies, rising property prices and technological advancements they have emerged as a successful and affluent generation. Many Baby Boomers are now settling into retirement, with many more luxuries and comforts in their golden years than experienced by generations before them.

Famous Examples:

Steve Jobs, Bill Gates, Sylvester Stallone, Bill Clinton, Donald Trump, George W Bush, Elton John, Lionel Richie, Richard Gere, Richard Branson, Mr T, David Hasselhoff, Liam Neeson, Steven Seagal, Pierce Brosnan.

Generation X

Generation X, came after the Baby Boomers, and typically covers people born between the mid 1960's and the early 1980's. Gen X was shaped by global political events that occurred during this generation's youth.

Events such as The Vietnam War, the fall of the Berlin Wall, the end of the Cold War, and the Thatcher-era government in the UK were events that helped to shape the culture and upbringing of Generation X. Relative to previous generations, Gen X is more open to diversity and has learnt to embrace differences such as religion, sexual orientation, class, race and ethnicity.

Famous Examples:

Charlie Sheen, Ben Stiller, Sarah Jessica Parker, Adam Sandler, David Cameron, Gordon Ramsay, Jennifer Lopez, Jay Z, Gwen Stefani, Matt Damon, Miranda Hart, Liam Gallagher, Robbie Williams, Victoria Beckham.

Generation Y

You guessed it, Generation Y came after Generation X. Generation Y covers people born between the 1980's and the year 2000, and these individuals are sometimes referred to as Gen Y, the Millennial Generation, or simply Millennials.

Generation Y has been shaped by the technological revolution that occurred throughout their youth. Gen Y grew up with technology, so being connected and tech savvy is in their DNA. Equipped with latest technology and gadgets, such as iPhones, laptops and smart devises, Generation Y is online and connected 24/7, 365 days a year.

Many Millennials grew up seeing their Baby Boomer parents working day and night doing stressful corporate jobs, which has shaped their own views on the workforce and the need for work-life balance. (They say, 'We are Millennials, and we understand ourselves better than anyone else!')

Famous Examples:

Kim Kardashian, Jessica Simpson, Jake Gyllenhaal, Macaulay Culkin, Beyoncé Knowles, Britney Spears, Justin Timberlake, Alicia Keys, Jessica Alba, Kate Middleton, Miranda Kerr, Keira Knightley, Usain Bolt, Zac Efron, Adele, Rihanna, Emma Watson, Ed Sheeran, Miley Cirus, Justin Bieber, Harry Styles.

Generation Z

Generation Z, is the generation of children born after the Year 2000. They are the children of Generation X and Generation Y. To be fair we don't know a whole lot about the character traits of Generation Z, because they haven't been on the earth for very long yet.

Generation Z are predicted to be highly connected, living in an age of high-tech communication, technology driven lifestyles and prolific use of social media. A lot of what we think we know about Generation Z is inferred, and only time will tell whether we have been correct.

Famous Examples:

Shiloh Jolie-Pitt, Suri Cruise, Blue Ivy Carter, Brooklyn Beckham, Apple Martin."[3]

Please note: discrepancies do exist with the years designated to each proclaimed cohort. You will notice this, as you undoubtedly fact-check, as I did, and you'll notice contradictions here and there. This is because everyone is making estimations and educated guesses.

No one really knows the "exact" start and finish dates for each demographic. It all depends on whom you talk to. It's a rather *fluid concept*. Nevertheless these demographics are approximately lumped into 15-20 year cohorts, so there is a general consensus, (give or take a year or five!)

Fuzzy Boundaries

To underscore this point, the Census Bureau, when pressed concerning the exact boundaries of each demographic answered: "We do not define the different generations... The only generation we do define is the Baby Boomers and that year bracket is from 1946 to 1964."

Philip Bump of The Atlantic contacted Tom DiPrete, (a sociology professor at Columbia University) with the same question. He answered: **"I think the boundaries end up getting drawn to some extent by the media... and the extent to which people accept them or not varies by the generation."**

I personally find this to be true, people view each demographic through the lens of their personal experiences or that of a loved one. Making it unique to them.

DiPrete explained that there was a good sociological reason for identifying the Baby Boom as a discrete generation. It "had specific characteristics," and occurred within an observable timeframe. World War II ended. You had the post-war rise in standard of living and the rise of the nuclear family. Then societal changes disrupted those patterns, and the generation, for academic purposes, was over. His main point: "History isn't always so punctuated."

DiPrete added, "I actually haven't seen efforts to document [generations] rigorously, and I would be somewhat sceptical that they can be documented rigorously." Observing that the things that have shaped Millennials — the rise of technology and social networks, for example — **"affect people's lives differently."**

He finished by saying, "The media in particular wants definitions, identities… **I don't know that the definitions are as strong or as widely shared across all the boundaries… At the end I think it gets fuzzy."**[4]

Therefore we must accept some of the "fuzziness" that comes with trying to understand demography. No one person or source has all the right answers; a lack of exactness and evident contradictions are *par-for-the-course,* with this particular subject unfortunately!

❖

CHAPTER 8

Avoiding Generational Cynicism

I t's easy for one generation to *despise* another, for various reasons. I want to discourage that. It's important that we harness what God wants to do in each and every generation. Not putting the older generations out to graze nor despising the youth that God is nurturing and raising up. If Timothy and Paul could work together, so can we.

Becoming cynical however is usually the result of losing sight of one's own purposes in life. The best example of this is Solomon who grew very cynical about life.

Yet God gave everything to Solomon with the prerequisite not to marry into paganism, however it was his boredom that made it easy for his hundreds of wives and concubines to seduce him with their foreign gods.

Steve Jobs was clever but mean. Solomon was clever and became cynical. He lost his purpose and intimacy therefore saw no purpose for the next generation. Cynicism's scornful indifference taunts with mocking whispers, *"What's the point?"*

Although Solomon possessed considerable knowledge and insight it was primarily his loss of focus that made him so pessimistic.

These are the words of the Quester, David's son and king in Jerusalem. Smoke, nothing but smoke. [That's what the Quester says.] There's nothing to anything — it's all smoke. What's there to show for a lifetime of work, a lifetime of working your fingers to the bone?

One generation goes its way, the next one arrives, but nothing changes — it's business as usual for old planet earth. The sun comes up and the sun goes down, then does it again, and again — the same old round... All the rivers flow into the sea, but the sea never fills up. The rivers keep flowing to the same old place, and then start all over and do it again.

Everything's boring, utterly boring - no one can find any meaning in it. Boring to the eye, boring to the ear. What was will be again, what happened will happen again. There's nothing new on this earth. Year after year it's the same old thing.

Does someone call out, "Hey, this is new"? Don't get excited — it's the same old story. Nobody remembers what happened yesterday. And the things that will happen tomorrow? Nobody'll remember them either. Don't count on being remembered...

I've said to myself, "I know more and I'm wiser than anyone before me in Jerusalem. I've stockpiled wisdom and knowledge." What I've finally concluded is that so-called wisdom and knowledge are mindless and witless — nothing but spitting into the wind.

(Ecclesiastes 1:1-11 MSG)

This is a warning to us all. If we can't see purpose in something, we are generally cynical towards it and we can't afford to be cynical towards what God is doing within another generation.

We are all called "...according to *His* purpose" not our own (Romans 8:28). It's imperative then that we see *God's* purpose or risk perishing in our own cynicism and lack of vision.

Once we see purpose in something, we can celebrate it. **But many in the world today only want to celebrate their own genius and success. This is toxic to unity.**

Regardless of fame, expertise or genius, anyone who can't celebrate the lives of others, will perish in the seduction of their own success, leaving it for others to inherit and enjoy, without them. **"Everything you have worked hard to acquire will end up in someone else's hands.** Your life will end with groanings *of remorse, of opportunities missed*, and your flesh and bones will be eaten up *with sorrow, regret for worthless efforts"* (Proverbs 5:10-11 VOICE).

High Minded Intolerance

Look at the PC culture today. Cynicism thrives. It's just packaged differently. Those who profess to be super "tolerant" and "politically correct" today usually only tolerate those views that line up with their own. The highly educated and sophisticated amongst us, still feel derision for anything intellectually inferior. So not much has changed.

Division and contempt for one another is on the rise generally. It's evident in all sectors of society not just politics. Consider this, as knowledge increases so does the contempt, therefore political correctness is just a veil for high-minded-intolerance.

At the time of writing this book, we've just come through some pretty major political upheavals around the globe. Elections in different nations have shown that when groups of faceless bureaucrats or elites try to govern the same population that they're out-of-touch with, things don't go as planned! When *"elites"* only breathe the same air as the few at the top, they lack the ability to relate with anyone outside of that bubble. Then wonder why they can't win elections by a landslide!

Definition: Bureaucrats refer to government officials who are concerned about ***procedural correctness*** *at the expense of people's needs.*

Such divisions have been highlighted across the globe and can't be underestimated. "A household divided against itself cannot stand" (Mark 3:25). This high-minded-intolerance must not enter the church. There must be a working together if we are to succeed, in our families, societies, in our nations and especially in the Body of Christ.

Intolerance can exist anywhere and manifest in many forms such as ageism, classism, sexism, fascism, able-bodyism, racism, anti-Semitism, even intellectualism and so on.

While I may not be writing a book about intolerance, I'm always concerned about how culture is impacting the church. (Later we discuss, Tolerance the god of this Age Sits on the Throne of Culture, so keep reading!)

❖

CHAPTER 9

Intellectual Intolerance is on the Rise

The wisdom from above is first pure [morally and spiritually undefiled], then peace-loving **[courteous, considerate]**, gentle, reasonable [and willing to listen], full of compassion and good fruits. It is unwavering, without [self-righteous] hypocrisy [and self-serving guile] (James 3:17 AMP).

As society is becoming more intelligent, you'd assume that intolerance would be diminishing. Yet intellectual intolerance is on the rise and like all intolerance, can be particularly cruel. I have two examples:

Sheldon: The short definition of intellectualism is: *the exercise of the intellect at the expense of the emotions.* Everything is based on reason. This reminds me of Theoretical Physicist Dr Sheldon Cooper from the hit TV series, "The Big Bang Theory." This fictional character is portrayed by actor Jim Parsons, whose portrayal of Dr Cooper, can be hilarious at times. While targeting other issues, the writers poke some good-natured fun at *intellectualism* and those who worship at the altar of reason and don't know how to be human, spontaneous or considerate.

Steve Jobs: On a more serious note let's consider Steve Jobs. While I love all things Apple Mac (because the Mac iOS has revolutionized my life!) and my appreciation of his genius is indisputable, I still must point out his meanness.

Jobs, is the perfect example of *intellectual intolerance.* He was a genius who couldn't suffer fools gladly and his open contempt for his intellectual inferiors was well documented.

One spokesperson said, "Steve Jobs was a… borderline sociopath. If you define that as someone who does evil things and doesn't feel remorse, the picture of a smirking Steve Jobs does begin to emerge.

Jobs was busy changing the world and minor annoyances like people's feelings didn't fit into his plan… People rallied around his genius and accepted his demands and abuse because Jobs really was smarter than everyone else in the room and 99.98 percent of the planet."[1]

Another said, "Jobs' merciless ways can also be tied to an intolerance of subpar employees… Jobs believed it was his 'job to be honest,' and that included tearing down an employee who didn't do something well enough."[2]

"Object of His Cruelty"

However it was Chrisann Brennan (Jobs' first girlfriend and the mother of his daughter Lisa) who wrote in her 2013 memoir called The Bite in the Apple, that she was "the object of his cruelty." She also published an essay in Rolling Stone, where she recollects their early free-spirited romance and the "all-too-often *despotic* jerk Steve turned into as he rose to meet the world."

Later her plea to Jobs' widow included: "Your loyalty to Steve does not mean loyalty to his hatreds… I simply never deserved the years of poverty and justifications he built up against me."[3]

Evidently those who possess incredibly high IQs don't always possess equally high EQs.

Definition: EQ refers to *emotional intelligence* or *emotional quotient:* the notional measure of a person's adequacy in such areas as self-awareness, empathy, and dealing sensitively with other people. Example, *"…she was described as a chilly elitist with the EQ of Mr Spock."*

Suffering Fools Gladly

To underpin this I found an article in the New York Times with the exact title, "Suffering Fools Gladly." Discussing the high-minded and highbrow intolerance of the elite, which included Mr Jobs.

Writer of the article David Brooks wrote: "Recently I was reading a magazine profile of a brilliant statistician. The article mentioned, in passing, that this guy doesn't *suffer fools gladly*. I come across that phrase a lot.

I've read that Al Gore and former Representative Barney Frank don't suffer fools gladly. Neither, apparently, did Steve Jobs, George Harrison, Pauline Kael or even Henry David Thoreau."

Interestingly Brooks gives credence to the bible by stating, "The phrase originally came from William Tyndale's 1534 translation of the bible. In it, Paul was ripping into the decadent citizens of Corinth for turning away from his own authoritative teaching and falling for a bunch of second-rate false apostles. **'For ye suffer fools gladly,'** Paul says with withering sarcasm, 'seeing ye yourselves are wise.'"

Ambiguous Compliment

He goes on to say, "Today, the phrase is often used as an ambiguous compliment. It suggests that a person is so smart he has trouble, tolerating people who are far below his own high standards.

It is used to describe a person who is so passionately committed to a vital cause that he doesn't have time for social niceties toward those *idiots* who stand in his/her way. It is used to suggest a level of social courage; a person who has the guts to tell idiots what he really thinks."

"Sure," he continues, "it would be better if such people were nicer to those around them, the phrase implies, but this is a forgivable sin in one so talented. This sounds fine in the abstract, but when you actually witness somebody in the act of not suffering fools gladly, it looks rotten.

Once I watched a senior member of the House of Representatives rip into a young reporter after she nervously asked him an ill-informed question. She was foolish about that particular piece of legislation, **but, in the moment, he looked the bigger fool...**

He was exposing a yawning gap between his own *high opinion of himself* and his actual conduct in the world. He was making the mistake, which metaphysical fools tend to make, that there is no connection between your inner moral quality and the level of courtesy you present to others."

He finishes by saying, "Politeness is a discipline that compels respectful behaviour... (Jane Austen was the novelist most famous for advocating this point of view). I don't give myself high marks on suffering fools. I'm not rude to those I consider foolish, but I strenuously and lamentably evade them. But I do see people who handle fools well. Many members of the clergy do, as do many great teachers..."[4]

The Pitfalls of Superior Intelligence

As a member of the clergy, this is a healthy reminder how people are more impacted by our behaviour than our beliefs. They don't want what we have until they can see that we care. Conduct sets us apart and classifies us as *the-adults-in-the-room,* who own calmness and composure, especially in trying situations. Scripture teaches us, "by their fruits ye shall know them" (See Matthew 7:15-20, Galatians 5:22).

However going back to Paul the apostle, I firmly believe that he was an *über intelligent* individual. He obviously understood the pitfalls of his superior intelligence, because he wrote: "If I… [possess] all knowledge… but do not have love [reaching out to others], I am nothing" (1 Corinthians 13:2 AMP).

There is a *lust* for knowledge today. A lust that is not new to humanity. Eve was seduced just by the *thought* of being all knowing like God. Imagine, all knowing, how delectable and enticing! The Internet opens up the gateway for knowledge and information like never before and now we can all feel like omniscient gods!

As believers do we share this lustful impulse to be godlike and all knowing?

We know that newer generations will be more knowledgeable than their forefathers (therein lies the threat). Yet striving for knowledge without knowing God's purposes will do for us what it did for Solomon. It will make us cold, cynical and judgmental. Still, when we espouse the knowledge that God (as master builder) gives us with His purposes, the results are always going to be innovative, redemptive, and creative.

Once again, Paul was well educated, but his life's work only became redemptive once he was *in* Christ. **Before his Damascus road experience Paul also had zero tolerance.** He was exhibit-A of religious intolerance! However, after being knocked from his high-horse by God, *everything* Paul did and taught was redemptive. Intelligence might be awesome, but it's how we treat others at the end of the day, that counts most.

Intergenerational Shifting

I want to be someone who is always able to see the value and potential in other people and celebrate it. I want to see what God is doing in different orbits, other than my own.

I want to see what God sees, in the fathers and sons of our society, in the spiritually mature and immature. While a generational divide might exist, it doesn't have to pose a threat. Instead of resisting change, we must see where God is in the change.

Where is God in all this intergenerational shifting? If we ask these questions and seek God like this, we will be better prepared to embrace and help instruct these newer generations, rather than trying to hide the fact that we are threatened by them. We have to posture ourselves much better than that.

❖

CHAPTER 10

Defining a Generation

So now let's focus on the Millennial cohort more specifically, who today range approximately between 18-34 years of age. And who represent that major voting and marketing block that everyone is feverishly trying to woo.

Not all Millennials enjoy being called Millennials however. To some it's an insult. So I'll do my level best to be positive towards Millennials and do them some justice. As the stereotype given them is not always flattering! For one example, Hillary Clinton, during her presidential campaign in 2016, was found calling them basement-dwellers, "who still live in their parents basement."

This didn't go down too well, as the fact of the matter is that just *one third* of Millennials are estimated to be still living at home with their parents, which means *most of them were not!* Many Millennials were angry at this inaccurate assessment of their entire demographic (some 80 million in America alone). So while courting their vote, it didn't help to offend them.

To add insult to injury the title "Millennial" has become synonymous with the word "narcissism." Millennials have consistently been acknowledged as the most narcissistic generation that has ever lived (ouch!)

"I'm so glad I never feel important, it does complicate life!"

– Eleanor Roosevelt

However I've become convinced that using such *one-size-fits-all* approach, or using such a *broad-brush* for labelling an entire generation is perhaps not the smartest thing to do and probably should be avoided.

America's Largest Generation

Various study groups cite differing numbers, but according to an article from FacTank in 2016, on the Pew Research Centre website, Millennials overtake Baby Boomers as America's largest generation. It says, "Millennials have surpassed Baby Boomers as the nation's largest living generation, according to population estimates released this month by the U.S. Census Bureau. Millennials, whom we define as those ages 18-34 in 2015, now number 75.4 million, surpassing the 74.9 million Baby Boomers (ages 51-69). And Generation X (ages 35-50 in 2015) is projected to pass the Boomers in population by 2028.

Notably the Millennial Generation continues to grow as young immigrants expand its ranks. Boomers – whose generation was defined by the boom in U.S. births following World War II – are older and their numbers shrinking as the number of deaths among them exceeds the number of older immigrants arriving in the country.

Generations are analytical constructs, and developing a popular and expert consensus on what marks the boundaries between one generation and the next takes time. Pew Research Centre has established that **the oldest Millennial was born in 1981.** The Centre continues to assess demographic, attitudinal and other evidence on habits and culture that will help to establish when the youngest Millennial was born or even when a new generation begins. To distil the implications of the census numbers for generational heft, this analysis assumes that **the youngest Millennial was born in 1997.**"[1]

The Good The Bad and The Ugly

Utilizing many different sources, we'll start with what the critics are saying about Generation Y and it's not pretty!

Incompetent:

One particular source refers to Millennials as: "A media popularized term for a generation of people born in western culture who came to adulthood in the early 21st century. **Often confused for being tech savvy or capable in life skills, Millennials are more often incapable with life skills** that earlier generations are commonly more adept at, such as changing car tires, filling out paperwork, hooking up entertainment centres or reading usage agreements and contracts on websites and smart phone apps before agreeing to them.

Millennials are more often only functional with contemporary front-end usage of modern technology while being confused and incapable with more practical applications and the service of hardware... **The Millennials are for the most part very deficient in common life skills, sustainability and practical capability."**

"I just saw a Millennial trying to change a tire and add oil to his car. He gave up after dumping transmission fluid in the oil intake and trying to jack his fender until it crumpled."[2]

What the critics say:

1. Millennials are just as racist as their elders
2. Millennials are the generation least informed about the news
3. Millennials are the nation's leading vaccine sceptics
4. Millennials care less about free speech than other generations
5. Millennials want special privileges
6. Millennials are job hoppers
7. Millennials are irresponsible
8. Millennials don't want to grow up
9. Millennials don't want to pay their own way
10. Millennials are over-dependent

11. Millennials are still living at home

12. Millennials are easily side-tracked by technology

13. Millennials want a trophy for showing up

14. Millennials are entitled, selfish and lazy

15. Millennials need constant approval and hand-holding

16. Millennials find criticism difficult

17. Millennials are narcissistic (self absorbed, ego driven, preoccupied)

18. Millennials are more irreligious and irreverent than previous generations

19. Millennials are addicted to technology but lack basic communication skills

20. Millennials are *over-informed-know-it-all's* and *practically* incompetent

21. Millennials are over opinionated and under qualified

22. Millennials are chronically over-rated

How Millennials Estimate Themselves

Clearly the critics view Millennials as entitled, selfish and lazy. Yet, when asked to distinguish themselves apart from other generations, here are some of their top responses.

In comparison to other demographics we are:

1. The most entrepreneurial

2. The most educated

3. We are the most tolerant

4. We have our priorities straight

5. We are the most independent thinkers

6. We love debunking the establishment and status quo

7. We are the most informed

8. The most technologically and socially connected

9. The most creative

10. The most authentic

11. We travel more

12. We feel younger for longer

13. We are the most relaxed about sex

14. We're having kids later or not at all

15. For us, experiences and making memories, mean more than stuff

16. We have a better grip on the work/life ratio. Money v. happiness

17. Exciting parts of the past are new to us, we can discover them at any time

18. Technology allows us to enjoy cultural DIY

19. We get to pick our own priorities

20. We're ridiculously resourceful

21. We don't smoke like our parents…

22. And for us mental health is as much of a priority as physical health

❖

CHAPTER 11

European Millennials

As addressed already, we know that approximately one third of Millennials in the US still live at home. However, where I live currently in Italy, that ratio is double that. Approximately two thirds stay at home. Again this refers to the 18-34 year olds. According to an online article written in the Italian section of The Local, in 2016: **"Two thirds of Italian Millennials live with their parents."**

The article said, "An increasing number of Italian youngsters are choosing - or have no other choice - to live at home with their parents, with less than a third of under-35's having flown the nest. Sixty-seven percent of 18-34-year-old Italians live with their parents, the latest figures from statistics agency Eurostat show, and a figure almost 20 points higher than the European average.

Meanwhile, in northern Europe, the vast majority of young adults live independently, 19.7 percent in Denmark, 34.3 percent in the UK and 34.5 percent in Germany.

Across Europe as a whole, the proportion of youngsters living at home has seen an overall drop since the 2008 recession. **But Italy bucks the trend; the percentage has crept up steadily each year,** with a notable increase of almost two points between 2014 and 2015.

Particularly notable is the high proportion (50.6 percent) of Italians aged 25-34 who live at home, a figure which has risen from 44 percent in 2011 and is almost 22 points above the European average, behind only Greece (53.4 percent). By contrast, in Denmark, just 3.7 percent of 25-34-year-olds live with their parents, compared to 10.1 percent in France and 39.1 percent in neighbouring Spain.

Italian men are particularly likely to stay in the parental home, accounting for 73.6 percent of the total between 18 and 34.

While high rates of youth unemployment are a likely cause, Eurostat notes that **40.3 percent of the Millennials living at home were full-time workers.** Students accounted for 18.8 percent of the total, while 24.3 percent were unemployed."[1]

These statistics are very interesting, in contrast an article in the UK entitled, "Home Invasion" from The Guardian in 2015, said the following about young people still living at home with their parents in England: "It has been dubbed the hotel of mum and dad but few guesthouses have such favourable terms. As the housing crisis bites, a fifth of young adults are staying in the family home until they are at least 26, and the same proportion are not paying a penny towards their keep."[2]

The Boomerang Generation

In addition there are those who are being coined, "The Boomerang-Kids" or "The Boomerang-Generation." Referring to adult offspring returning to the nest after leaving for university and/or other.

Wikipedia gives this definition: "Boomerang Generation is a term applied to the current generation of young adults in Western culture. They are so named for the frequency with which they choose to share a home with their parents after previously living on their own – thus boomeranging back to their place of origin."[3]

Not all Millennials are Created Equal

So having said all this, *what of it?* The point is not all Millennials are created equal. Some fit the stereotype while others don't. For example, some are educated and have left home to become professionals while others have left home to raise their own families. Still others are just returning to the nest, while others have never left.

There are European Millennials that differ from one another and there are American Millennials that differ again. So can we paint them all with one big brush? I don't think so. In addition, some don't like to be labelled at all. Understandably. As we've seen, not all stereotypical descriptions are flattering!

Nonetheless we must keep asking probing questions to help with our perceptions. Such as: how is God moving amongst Millennials? What about church going Millennials, are they only taken seriously if they initiate themselves into Hillsongs-United? (Just a rhetorical question - wink!)

What is God saying to this particular cohort? How can they fulfil their mission and how can we help instruct them - to get it done? Have we become exhausted and obsolete while they remain energised? Or can we add our experience and expertise to their vitality and enthusiasm?

It's all thought provoking and life is not, by any means, going to slow down. The pace is only going to accelerate. Either we keep up or we don't.

What can we add to the Millennials that they don't already have? No generation is complete in and of itself. No matter how savvy or technically native it may seem. Let's aim to complete one another, as God intended.

Enter: "The Nones"

I've noticed of late, how the secular mainstream media have been obsessing over the rise of the *nones*. A term used to refer to individuals who are *unaffiliated* with any particular organized group or religion. Basically they consist of all those who tick the box, "none of the above" when filling out forms, or participating in surveys regarding religious affiliation.

Concerning this new phenomenon Pastor Rick Warren says, "The Millennial Generation is asking the right questions about life. They are spiritually hungry. They are looking for a transcendent purpose and real community. **While media has focused on the rise of the 'Nones,' it has ignored the outbreaks of spiritual revival among this age group across America."**

Totally turning popular opinion up on its head, he continues by saying, **"The world, as a whole, is becoming more devout, not more secular.** The recent Pew Research Centre study revealed that around the world the 'unaffiliated' group will grow by about 100,000,000 people between 2010 and 2050. **But the Christian church will grow by 750,000,000 in the same period—seven times faster—which will actually decrease the percentage of 'nones' on the planet."**[4]

Good news from Pastor Rick. Let's stick with the facts. All this new terminology isn't as intimidating as it sounds!

❖

CHAPTER 12

Gatekeepers in the Information and Digital Age

To begin with here is a short definition of what we will be talking about in this particular chapter - the information age and information technology:

"The information age (aka the computer age, digital age, or new media age) is a period in human history characterized by the shift from traditional industry that the industrial revolution brought through industrialization, to an economy based on information computerization.

The onset of the information age is associated with the digital revolution, just as the industrial revolution marked the onset of the industrial age. **During the information age, the phenomenon is that the digital industry creates**

a knowledge-based society surrounded by a high-tech global economy..."[1]

The acronym I.T. stands for information technology and it refers to anything related to computing technology, such as networking, hardware, software, the Internet, or the people that work with these technologies.

"Many companies now have IT departments for managing their computers, networks, and other technical areas of their businesses. IT jobs include computer programming, network administration, computer engineering, Web development, technical support, and many other related occupations. **Since we live in the 'information age,' information technology has become a part of our everyday lives.** That means the term 'IT,' already highly overused, is here to stay."[2]

The Gatekeepers

It would be hard for anyone to deny the vast acceleration in advancements being made all over the globe today, particularly in the fields of science and technology. Especially and not excluding Israel, which has become internationally recognised as a unique **hub of innovation** and is leading the world in many fields of expertise, especially in science and technology.

Such global advancements include that of information technology. We can agree that little travels faster than *information* today. With the invention of Twitter for example, gossip can go around the globe ten times, before you even get out of bed in the morning! In fact information technology on every level, whether scientific or social, has reached dizzying heights.

Well known for his teaching on eschatology Pastor John Hagee cites Daniel: "But you, Daniel, shut up the words, and seal the book till the time of the end; **many shall run to and fro, and knowledge shall increase**" (Daniel 12:4). Describing this as an explosion Pastor Hagee says, "a literal translation of this Scripture indicates that during the end time, or the terminal generation, **an explosion of knowledge will occur."**

This is consistent with the definition already given previously that said, "During the Information Age, the phenomenon is that the digital industry **creates a knowledge-based society** surrounded by a high-tech global economy…"

In addition to this, while out jogging recently, I listened to a podcast by Kris Vallotton, one of the prophetic voices coming out of Bethel church, in Redding California. He made the following statements that caught my attention:

"For thousands of years the planet was dominated by military tyrants who ruled the world. Next the religious mountain ruled the world largely through the Catholic church. In the industrial age we moved into the golden rule; 'he who has the gold, rules,' as large corporations dominated the world. Power was bought and sold for a price. **But in the information age, those who control the information gates: media, entertainment and social networking, rule the world."**

Ruling the World via Information

I have to agree with his sentiments on this; it's a solid point. One example of this was during the 2016 presidential campaign in the US, where we witnessed unadulterated bias along with blatant *misinformation,* which became known as "fake news." The media abuses and unfair "pile-on" against her opponent, were evident for all to see. Unashamedly partisan reporting revealed that journalism in America had died a death!

No longer a profession that seeks to keep politicians accountable (better known as an adversarial-press), journalists instead were overwhelmingly in-the-tank for their favoured candidate (Mrs Clinton), while displaying a collective loathe and hatred for the other.

Nevertheless it was "shock-and-awe" all around when this said "loathed" candidate actually won, against all the odds! Of course I am referring to now President Donald Trump. Revealing that the mass-manipulation-of-information (propaganda and fake-news) along with the overuse of celebrities, didn't provide the win-win that the liberal-left felt entitled to. In fact Trump was and still is an anathema to them.

However, many still believe in divine intervention, "If my people, which are called by my name, shall humble themselves, and pray, and seek my face, and turn from their wicked ways; then will I hear from heaven, and will forgive their sin, and will heal their land" (2 Chronicles 7:14 KJV).

With prayer back in the White House, divine intervention is certainly what we need. As time progresses we will see an increasing spiritual struggle over our "information-gateways." **Anyone trying to rule the world today certainly**

needs to invest in and look to conquer this particular gateway first, as a matter of priority.

In Ephesians 2:2 "…the prince of the power of the air," describes Satan who undoubtedly wants to control the "air-waves" which have traditionally been recognised as television and radio. Now we can add the Internet to that and so on but the fact remains, the information gateways are capable of propagating lies, falsehood, deceit, hatred and of course *very* fake news.

> *You belong to your father, the devil, and you want to carry out your father's desires. He was a murderer from the beginning, not holding to the truth, for there is no truth in him.* **When he lies, he speaks his native language, for he is a liar and the father of lies.**
>
> *(John 8:44 NIV)*

❖

CHAPTER 13

Waging Lawfare

In today's world lawfare, not traditional warfare, is the most effective and preferred *modus operandi* for destroying one's opponents, (business, political or other).

Definition: "Lawfare is a form of asymmetric warfare, consisting of using the legal system against an enemy, such as by damaging or delegitimizing them, tying up their time or winning a public relations victory. The word is a portmanteau of the words *law* and *warfare...*"[1]

Controlling the information gates means that you can control the people, right? Yet even though that sounds airtight and simple, it's deflated by the fact that today's society is less trusting of information and its sources, than ever before and has adapted itself radically. In fact a general public who now fact-checks EVERYTHING, is the new norm, including making their own news.

Citizen journalism is now mainstream media's biggest competitor. Bloggers, and twitter-trolls and the like, are fast, dangerous, unprofessional and pithy. They are no less political but perhaps much less *scripted* and edited by big media, which helps make them seem more authentic and *trustworthy* to their audience.

Now I don't suggest that the mainstream media or the professional press are in any immediate danger, because they're not. It's part of democracy to have an adversarial press. Only, now they have a healthy and robust new rival to help keep them on their toes.

No longer can they enjoy deceiving a deliberately *dumbed-down* audience, who believe everything they're told! But have to contend with a politically active society, on the whole.

And yes! Everyone suffers with *campaign-fatigue* at times, especially after a long and gruelling political season. However the world has just woken up to a new reality that the world we live in is now *constantly* campaigning, in other words this season will never end!

Everyone has become a political activist. Not just the media, but schoolteachers, bankers, students and even children. We live in a politically charged global village. It's only natural then, that with all the technology to hand, everyone wants to report the facts as *they* see them.

Definition: "The concept of citizen journalism (also known as public, participatory, democratic, guerrilla or street journalism) is based upon public citizens playing an active role in the process of collecting, reporting, analysing, and disseminating news and information."

According to Courtney C. Radsch citizen journalism can be defined, "as an alternative and activist form of newsgathering and reporting that functions outside mainstream media institutions, often as a response to shortcomings in the professional journalistic field, that uses similar journalistic practices but is driven by different objectives and ideals and relies on alternative sources of legitimacy than traditional or mainstream journalism."

Jay Rosen proposes a simpler definition of citizen journalism saying that it refers to, "...when the people formerly known as the audience employ the press tools they have in their possession to inform one another."

"Citizen journalism is not to be confused with community journalism or civic journalism, both of which are practiced by professional journalists. Collaborative journalism is also a separate concept and is the practice of professional and non-professional journalists working together."[2]

In addition more people today are becoming authors and self-publishing, at the utter dismay of professional book publishers. Why? Fewer restrictions, less expense and arguably less accountability too - perhaps.

However, a savvier society means that more people want to be gatekeepers of their own information. The fight is on. Everyone is contending for control of the same gateway. If you can control the information you can control the people. Information is power. But in the wrong hands, it spells destruction.

If people are armed with the right information, then more power to them! If however the information is censored or restricted this presents a lengthier discussion, like the threat of a censored Internet for example. However it's suffice to say, that fewer and fewer people are willing to be told how to think by big media and want to self-advocate.

The Thought Police of a PC Culture

Times have changed and the liberal **"thought-police"** who have made a living out of telling people how and what to think – must now change their tactics. One example to prove that general sentiments have changed is the over-use of celebrities in politics. Once used to help woo and reinforce votes, now only manages to annoy and insult the voter's intelligence instead.

We see today liberal thinkers and globalists scrambling to re-energise their message and re-strategizing their tactics after voters didn't jump through their political hoops. They suffered crushing defeats after Brexit – Britain leaving Europe and the Trump victory in the States.

The alleged "One World Order," that is trying to establish itself everywhere is being challenged. Including the ever-nervous (under constant threat of destabilization), European Union, that perhaps finally recognises society has changed.

The more *informed* a society is, the harder it is to control or persuade them to think in a box; unless you brain wash them constantly with bias and parochial information.

I am convinced that the all-out-liberal-pile-on of propaganda and the negative-information-overload that we are constantly bombarded with has backfired and forced many people to think for themselves and make up their own minds. Which is a very dangerous concept for a global government who wants to control them!

Attempts, as we speak, are constantly being made to censor the Internet. It's only a matter of time. Our freedoms of speech and religion are under continual threat. *Remember you can't control a people unless you control their information.*

The Internet as we know it, is already changing. Subtle censorship has already begun. One example of this is the recent introduction of "fake-news-alerts," on such platforms as Facebook and others. But let me ask you – who really dictates what's fake information and what isn't?

I suggest that such ploys represent a clever way of convincing people that they still have some control, when really they have none.

Bastions of Free Speech v. Book Burning

Sometimes those who threaten freedom of speech and those who defend it can be equally as unpredictable. Take college and university campuses, for example, that used to be safe places of, and bastions for, free speech. Now campuses resemble more of a platform where political activists, acting as professors, can program the next generation with their own political agendas. I strongly suggest that such professors need to distinguish the difference between conducting classes versus indoctrinating cult meetings!

Comedian Bill Maher came out in defense of conservative speaker Ann Coulter who was invited to speak at the UC Berkeley, which supposedly is the birthplace of the free speech movement. However Ms Coulter never did get to speak at Berkeley because of the political fallout that ensued.

Matt Vespa wrote in an online article from the Town Hall, "The latest victim in University of California, Berkeley's war against free speech: Ann Coulter. Yes, we all know that the Left views her as a succubus. Yes, we all know that she can be offensive to some people. And yes, she has the right to voice those opinions under the First Amendment, something that the Left seems to have forgotten. The irony is that UC Berkeley used to be a bastion of free speech. Now, it's a stronghold for shutting down such constitutionally protected activities, specifically for those who happen to have a contrary opinion to the unhinged ethos of progressivism today. It's a fortress of illiberalism.

Bill Maher may not be a fan of Coulter politically, but he certainly is not one who supports this nonsense. **On his show Real Time, he described the school as devolving from being a cradle for free speech into a 'cradle for** (*expletive removed*) **babies.'**

Maher, a friend of Coulter, made it known that he likes her as a person — but never agreed with her on anything. The HBO host also remembered when he was invited to speak at the school, which drew controversy since Maher doesn't buy the liberal narratives on Islam and radical Islamic terrorism. Some might find his opinions politically incorrect. He was disinvited, but then eventually allowed to come and speak. **Still, the pattern disturbed him.**

'This goes on all over the country on campuses. They invite someone to speak, who is not exactly what liberals want to hear, and they want to shut her down. **I feel like this is the liberals' version of book burning. It's got to stop.'** Maher said...

Maher is no conservative, but he understands (and respects) the importance of free speech, even for those he is diametrically opposed to in politics. **'That's what the First Amendment means. It doesn't mean just shut up and agree with me,'** he said."[3]

❖

CHAPTER 14

What comes first
the Chicken or the Egg?

Indeed. What comes first, in this information age, knowledge or experience, theory or practice? In yesteryear you were encouraged to learn by experience, now not so much. Information holds more weight. So if information is more valuable than experience, this influences the outcome of a generation.

In the case of the Millennials, they got the information before the experience and had the theory before the practice. When generations before them faced life the opposite way around. They lived the experience before they were given the knowledge or information to back it up. So since the information age, life has been turned on its head!

Now Millennials and everyone else for that matter, with access to knowledge through the speed of the computer connected to the Internet, can learn about every new experience, as it happens. They are so much better connected and informed than we were.

This means that Millennials, who have been exposed to knowledge and information at an earlier age, have had such vast opportunities, to learn. As a result knowledge and information has greatly increased.

Go back just 10 years for example, and the knowledge that's been gleaned in just one decade, would have taken many decades to glean. Now however, at the click of a button, you can be anywhere in the world.

You can fact check everything in real time, and why wouldn't you? As a result you can become very knowledgeable about anything in particular, practically instantly, even though you have had zero experience.

Unlimited Knowledge

You can learn how to build your own house, cut your own hair, fly a plane, get work-out and medical advice, speak different languages, learn high-end cooking skills and the list is endless. Information overload can cause some negative side effects of course, such as know-it-all's who know nothing by experience. **Instead they inflict everyone else with analysis paralysis!**

And yet when you go back before the time of the Millennials, to the Baby Boomer Generation, they were experiencing the natural side of life before they ever became really serious about gaining any factual aspects of life.

My husband says about the Boomers: "We were sort of letting our hair down, we were still hippies and the way that culture was at that time was more about, 'Let's enjoy life now and figure it out later!'"

So to my point, Millennials are not the only group that have researched, it's just that they started sooner, younger. My husband says of this, "They were initiated into the information age long before we ever were. They are natives! They grew up with all this technology at their fingertips, where my brothers and I started out playing in the mud with sticks and stones. We had to be inventive and create our own entertainment.

In addition the education wasn't there. You could get your hands on books at a library perhaps. Or the family would inherit a set of encyclopaedias from the grandparents. But these days you're encouraged to research and the information is much more readily available. It's at your fingertips, in picture form or even video, so that you cannot only read the information but see and hear knowledge at such an early age."

Experience v. Inexperience

Yet at some point you still need to *experience* life. It's not a spectator sport. It can't all be theory and no practice. Going to the amazon rain forest, for example, might not be on your bucket list, because you can see it better on a screen and pay less than a round trip. Yet life is still something to be touched and felt, not just viewed through a safe and remote cyber lens of convenience.

Exposure to knowledge and facts is awesome. I wouldn't want to live in an Internet black out, would you? Still, life-experience is crucial. The concept of *wisdom* reinforces this, which is different to mere knowledge and information. We can't live on information alone.

Wisdom requires experience, facts and time. Scripture honours old age. Length of days is something to be proud of, although it's the *experience* that really counts. "The glory of young men is their strength; **of old men, their experience**" (Proverbs 20:29 TLB). "Silver hair is a beautiful crown found in a righteous life" (Proverbs 16:31 GW).

When you explain your life to someone, you are explaining your experience not just information. Life is for living. Filling out a curriculum vitae or resume involves life-experience not just black typeset on a white page. What achievements you've secured and what schools you attended, including any travel and work-experience. Words alone don't impress.

10 Surprising Stats and Facts about this Digital Age

According to Erik Qualman, author of the book Socialnomics, who talks about stats and facts related to the digital age, gives the following 10 surprising facts:

1. Generations Y and Z consider email passé: Some universities have even stopped issuing email addresses to students

2. 92 percent of children under the age of 2 have digital shadows

3. If Wikipedia were made into a book, it would be 2.25 million pages

4. 90 percent of customers trust peer recommendations compared with 14 percent who trust advertising

5. Facebook's 1 billion members makes it the third largest nation in the world (behind China and India)

6. Every day, 20 percent of Google searches have never been searched for in the past

7. Social media has become the No. 1 activity on the Web

8. One in five couples meet online; three in five gay couples meet online

9. One in five divorces are blamed on Facebook

10. The Ford Explorer launch on Facebook created more traffic than a Super Bowl ad[1]

However things do tend to come full circle again, eventually. As now Millennials, are out for adventure, in the real world. They want to download *experiences,* rather than information, in real-time. Recent studies show that Millennials are prioritizing experiences over stuff. In fact a study by Harris Group found that "72 percent of Millennials prefer to spend more money on experiences than on material things.

They're prioritizing on cars and homes less and less, and assigning greater importance to personal experiences and then showing off pictures of them. For fear of missing out they aren't spending money on cars, TVs and watches so much as renting scooters and touring Vietnam, rocking out at music festivals, or hiking Machu Picchu."[2]

In fact they're turning in vast numbers to things such as vinyl records, simply because they're experiencing them for the first time. Preferring to hold something tangible in their hands opposed to just downloading a song or album title onto their computer screens. Holding the album cover in their hands makes them feel more *involved* in the process and can appreciate the artwork, close up. This is a new world - for some.

❖

CHAPTER 15

Young Digital Shadows and Fatal Preoccupation

The most fascinating on the list for me was number 2, which said, "92 percent of children under the age of 2 have digital shadows." So what is a digital shadow? It's talking about an Internet footprint, also known as a "cyber shadow or electronic footprint." Referring to the information that's left behind as a result of a user's web-browsing (stored as cookies). And anyone can have a "digital shadow," whether individuals, businesses, organisations or corporations.

All this new jargon! Many are talking about things like the need for digital hygiene and how they have grown up in a digital fishbowl. Times change and so does the language!

No Limitations

If you go way back in the day, bibles were withheld from laymen and women in the pews, because the general population were illiterate. So they had to go to church to have someone read the Word of God to them. Including the synagogues. People would spend hours there, listening to someone else reading out loud.

There was simply no alternative way of getting the information they needed. Now however, besides having leather bound, gold edged bibles in our possession, we also have available to us modern bible applications on our smart devises that have audio bibles. How times have changed. We have no excuse!

Then considering such notable figures like Churchill and Eleanor Roosevelt who were both involved in politics, they were raised during a period when access to the best schools and education was reserved for those in the aristocracy, who had the means to pay for it.

Access to knowledge was a privilege and those who enjoyed such education had an obligation to "give back," and many of them were expected to go into politics. So unless you were educated you could not progress in society to any great height. It was limited to those who had access to the right information.

Thankfully access to knowledge and information is no longer reserved for aristocracy. All of us have free access to the Internet regardless of our upbringing. The limits are off and the sky is the limit. For instance one of my husband's favourite shows on UK television is, "Grand Designs" with Kevin McCloud.

Amongst the most ostentatious designs, were couples who had learnt to build their homes entirely off the Internet, converting cowsheds into cosy living spaces! **What will the children of tomorrow be able to achieve?**

It's not uncommon today for 5 year olds to have their own computers, devices (iPads), or even smart phones. But I agree with Erik Qualman, author of "Socialnomics," because our youngest daughter was already a competent user of her mummy's iPad and iPhone by the age of 2. (We have photos!) And growing up with all this stuff around them and available to them, children today have a totally different worldview than we did.

She will never know life without a smart device. It's literally from birth. Children are learning numbers and the alphabet online before they ever go to pre-school. They're even being encouraged by conscientious parents to learn two or three different languages, before the age of six when it's estimated that children are most receptive.

Preoccupation in the Smart Age

The point is that smart devices have become our lives. When my husband gave me my first iPhone, it literally changed my world. I organize my entire life that way. And now my whole family has them. Our youngest is not ten yet, and still she has her own iPhone, mini iPad, and can operate a computer. Times have changed.

The fact is that smart phones have changed all of our lives. Once I heard a well-known comedian talk about how he liked to "people-watch," in particular how people dealt with the panic and loss of misplacing their cell phones. (Keeping in mind that all their personal information is on there). It's the modern lamentation: "My entire life is on that phone!" Compare this to the lost handbag. Most women can't remember what's in their handbag, but their life depends on it! And this comedian went so far as to say, "They panic more about losing a device than their own child!"

Comedy aside, I've seen adults crossing busy roads with small children in toe behind them, yet completely oblivious to their safety. Instead of their attention being on their children, they're looking down at their cell phone. It's totally inappropriate. There's a time and a place for everything but checking your Facebook feed, while crossing the road with small children, is irresponsible.

We only see the top of people's foreheads these days, because no one's looking up anymore. It's the heads-down generation and the very tools, which can improve our lives, also endanger them. Cell-phone-over-use and addiction is dangerous; as accidents are happening everywhere including hospitals, care centres and even railway lines.

One big example of this was the train crash in Santiago de Compostela, Spain, when it was revealed that the driver responsible was on his phone moments before the accident. Which added to growing concerns among regulators worldwide about the pernicious consequences of phone use while operating vehicles, trains and planes. **The crash was**

Spain's most deadly in decades, with 79 people killed and 66 hospitalised with injuries.

Investigation into what happened showed that the driver, Francisco Jose Garzon Amo, was on the phone as the train sped up to 121 mph before derailing. Investigators said Amo received three warnings to reduce his speed in the minutes leading up to the crash.

"**'Distracted driving is an epidemic.** It is dangerous, deadly and irresponsible when operating any type of transportation equipment,' Joseph Szabo, the federal railroad administrator, told **The Huffington Post.** 'That is why we have banned the unauthorised use of electronic devices while operating freight or passenger trains and why many railroads also have adopted strict operating rules against the practice.'"[1]

Then there was the woman who mowed down and killed a 70-year-old man because she was logged into Facebook at the time of the accident. The woman in question was **updating her Facebook page** via mobile phone at the same time that she placed a call for emergency roadside assistance.

Another driver was found paying bills via her cell phone at the same time she collided with the car in front of her, which burst into flames and resulting in the death of the passenger. This driver was sentenced to six years in prison.[2]

So this is the new phenomena that we're now dealing with in the smart-age. The more technology we have, the less responsibility we show and the more distracted we have become, both at work and at home. **Compromised safety should never be the fruit of modern technology.**

❖

CHAPTER 16

The War between Religion and Science

To continue, much good comes from innovation, technology and science. Contrary to popular belief the church is not at war with science and common sense! A charge that goes way back to the times of Galileo, The Father of Science, who in the 16th century was *allegedly* convicted of heresy (trying to reinterpret the bible) by the Catholic church, for claiming that the earth was round and not flat. When actually the true controversy stemmed from his defence of heliocentrism.

The heliocentric theory claimed that the sun, not the earth, was at the centre of the universe and that the earth orbits the sun, not the other way around. Which at the time, appeared to contradict certain passages of scripture.

It is argued by the Catholic church today that the idea that the church dogmatically opposed the new science and even had Galileo tortured is somewhat disingenuous and not entirely accurate: **"In reality, the church was the leading sponsor of the new science and Galileo himself was funded by the church. The leading astronomers of the time were Jesuit priests.** They were open to Galileo's theory but told him the evidence for it was inconclusive."

As for the flat earth fallacy, "According to the atheist narrative, the medieval Christians all believed that the earth was flat until the brilliant scientists showed up in the modern era to prove that it was round. In reality, educated people in the Middle Ages knew that the earth was round.

In fact, the ancient Greeks in the fifth century B.C. knew the earth was a globe. They didn't need modern science to point out the obvious. They could see that when a ship went over the horizon, the hull and the mast disappear at different times. Even more telling, during an eclipse they could see the earth's shadow on the moon."

Politically Invented Caricature

As we've all heard of fake-news today, it's not hard to realise that false information is nothing new! Fake-history then also comes into play. In fact misinformation has helped shape history, as we know it. But who is right and who is wrong?

Although many would see their vested interest in opposing what is now considered common knowledge, according to the Catholic church, any claims that Galileo was a victim of torture and abuse, should be seen as a myth that was invented by the left and something that has long been debunked:

"This is perhaps the most recurring motif, and yet it is entirely untrue. **Galileo was treated by the church as a celebrity. When summoned by the Inquisition, he was housed in the grand Medici Villa in Rome.**

He attended receptions with the Pope and leading cardinals. Even after he was found guilty, he was first housed in a magnificent Episcopal palace and then placed under 'house arrest' although he was permitted to visit his daughters in a nearby convent and to continue publishing scientific papers."

In addition to this and to further debunk any myth or false narrative, D'Souza quotes historian Gary Ferngren who alleged, **"...the traditional picture of Galileo as a martyr to intellectual freedom and as a victim of the church's opposition to science has been demonstrated to be little more than a caricature."**[1]

Although not in perfect alliance, UCLA's Research Professor Henry Kelly is still quoted as saying, "Many people believe that Galileo was hounded by the church for almost two decades, that he openly maintained a belief in heliocentrism, and that he was only spared torture and death because his powerful friends intervened on his behalf. But an examination of the fine details of Galileo's conflict with church leaders doesn't bear that out...

After his formal trial, which took place on May 10 of that year (1633), Galileo was convicted of a 'strong suspicion of heresy,' a lesser charge than actual heresy... In sum, the 1616 event was not the beginning of a 17-year-long trial, as is often said, but a non-trial... Galileo's actual trial lasted for only a fraction of a single day, with no fanfare at all."[2]

So scholars and researchers continue to disagree on historical facts. Gaps are usually filled by educated guesses and influenced by differing ideologies. Besides even if there were political reasons for the Orthodox church to oppose innovation in the past, it's certainly not doing it now. In fact true believers in the body of Christ should be catalysts and promoters for the arts, innovation, science and technology.

Israeli Innovation is Leading the World

We can say that our faith is not threatened by science, rather confirmed by it, right? Thankfully today we celebrate innovation more than ever before, with Israel at the very centre of it, as previously mentioned. So clearly God uses innovation and we are not afraid of it. Just think, if He was against it, then He certainly forgot to inform Israel, who have collectively become the sharpest tool in His shed (wink again!)

According to the following article, "How Did Israel Become a Hub for Innovation?" this is the question many are asking around the world today. Author and Israeli, Tzahi Weisfeld gives his perspective: "In the past year, Israeli startups enjoyed exits — meaning acquisitions and initial public offerings — worth about $15 billion, an all-time record, according to Forbes...

For centuries, the Jewish people who started this nation had to run, hide, and fight to survive. They had to stand up for themselves when no one else did. So they did the only thing that made sense and transformed challenges into assets.

The land is arid — they excel at water and agricultural technology. There are no resources — they developed alternatives for fuel. Israel is surrounded by enemies, so its military technology is superb, and it inspires further innovation.

Israelis had to learn how to work well under pressure, and since they had no other alternative, they turned adversity into a source of competitive advantage.

Mandatory military service for both men and women has had a big impact on Israel's entrepreneurial culture. At 16, hackers and math prodigies are handpicked to undergo elite training that will give them extensive knowledge and experience in the most relevant technologies..."[3]

Being Part of the Nerd Herd

Whether you are a Millennial or not I encourage you to embrace the change and to see the rapid advancements in science and technology as positive, not as an necessary evil. In fact let's join the nerd herd! Technology, science and innovation are all tools that we must utilize for Jesus. So how do we do that?

We must use all the methods and vehicles available to spread and transport His message, while there's still time and freedom to do so. We're no longer limited to the donkey system of travel, from eras past. No! We have much more sophisticated and speedier modes of transportation these days and even faster ways of transporting information. So we *must* use them.

Using I.T. to Reach - "All the World"

So the most effective way of getting the message out there today involves information technology or I.T as it's best known. An explosive industry that just keeps ramping up and evolving at such speed that it's pretty hard keeping up - no matter how savvy we think we are.

The Internet as we know, is a vast resource in our hands and we can be as resourceful as we want to be. But it all comes down to motives. While greed and other influences do utilize the Internet, our main purpose is spreading the good news and proclaiming the kingdom of God.

Let's be clear, if Jesus were roaming the earth today, He wouldn't be doing so on a donkey! He'd be using the same modes of transportation that we do and using the same tools of technology. God himself made the Internet available, to aid us in our quest, more than anything else, of fulfilling this Great Commission:

> Go into **all the world** and preach and **publish openly** the good news (the Gospel) to every creature (of the whole human race).
>
> (Mark 16:15 AMP)

Walking through these different generational cohorts reveals our stark differences as we all contend for the great commission laid out in Mark 16 above. One thing is abundantly clear - we must work together.

Someone will say, "Yes but is all this talk on generational cohorts necessary or relevant? Jesus never talked about such things. He just preached about the kingdom. We should do the same." I agree. Without labelling them, Jesus managed to reach every people group, because **He understood their needs.** He spoke their language. He reached them. No barriers, whether religion, sickness or age.

His truth will always be for **"...all the world."**

❖

CHAPTER 17

Generation X

Definition of Generation X (Gen Xers 1960's to 1980's): Sometimes I feel as though this particular cohort has become the forgotten generation; barely mentioned and certainly not sharing any spotlight with the Millennials Generation.

So just briefly I will touch on this particular cohort, but I don't want to linger here long. Yet, as I have each demographic cohort represented in my personal family, each cohort is of great interest to me.

As with any, the brush is broad and long that tries to portray and stereotype Gen-X and not all characteristic labels ring true. For me, it's mainly the references to differences in technology and opportunity that are the most important distinctions to make between the generations.

Consistent with many sources Generation X refers to the generation born after that of the Baby Boomers (roughly from the early 1960s to early 1980s), and were typically perceived to be *disaffected* and *directionless*. But one major factor to me is that Generation X grew up with I.T (information technology).

The Middle Child of Generations

According to an article in Forbes Magazine in 2014 entitled, **"Generation X: Once Xtreme, Now Exhausted,"** it says the following: "Generation X (born 1961-81) today comprises roughly 87 million adults in their 30s and 40s. The very name 'X' has an identity-cloaking quality, reflecting the fact that many Xers feel little generational centre of gravity.

They are, first of all, the most immigrant generation per capita born in the 20th century. They are also the most unequal — that is, the most spread out in terms of income and wealth."[1]

According to Pew Research Centre Gen X "...are projected to remain the 'middle child' of generations – caught between two larger generations of the Millennials and the Boomers... smaller than Millennials... Gen Xers were born during a period when Americans were having fewer children than later decades.

When Gen Xers were born, births averaged around 3.4 million per year, compared with the 3.9 million annual rate during the 1980s and 1990s when Millennials were born."[2]

The Greatest Anti-child Phase in Modern History

Another interesting factor about Gen-X is brought to light by author of "Are You There, God? It's Me, Generation X," Jennifer McCollum who says, "Today, there are well over 50 million members of Generation X. We are sometimes referred to as *Baby Busters* because our birth years follow the baby boom that began after World War II.

That boom began to decline in 1957 and was further hastened by FDA approval of oral contraceptives in 1960. By 1965, 6.5 million women were on 'the pill' and in 1973, abortion was legalized."

Obviously she is citing specific numbers relevant to America, but as we know, America has always influenced the rest of the world. Known for its patriotism, the US has long labelled itself, "the free world" and/or "the most advanced democracy on earth."

The trickle down effect on the rest of the world however, has not always been advantageous. As Jennifer continues by saying, **"Generation X was born during the greatest anti-child phase in modern American history.** Our childhoods were underscored by the following:

- Legalized Abortion (Roe v. Wade)
- Invention of Birth Control
- Divorce
- Absent Fathers
- Working Mothers
- Latchkey Kids

Facebook is Dominated by Gen X not Gen Y

Numbers prove, against popular assumption, that Gen Xers dominate Facebook not Millennials. And apart from growing up in the shifting changes of I.T. and popularized abortion, here McCollum gives some additional stereotypical traits given to Generation X:

"Adrift, Apathetic and Cynical: In youth and childhood, Generation X was often described as being adrift. The archetype of loner emerged. In reality, members, especially young men, were *disenfranchised* by a loss of familial support and later technology. Think: Video Games. In adulthood, the introspective, disconnected Gen-Xer has re-engaged through social media.

We've discovered that our stories aren't unique. In fact, the narratives are strikingly similar. **Facebook is dominated by Generation X and through millions of status updates we've discovered our shared history, our shared secrets.**"[3]

So there *is* one good thing about Facebook then! That, while Millennials were migrating away from Facebook, a former disenfranchised generation located themselves and *reconnected* on Facebook.

❖

CHAPTER 18

The Landmark Decision of Roe v. Wade

In the previous chapter I very briefly mentioned the subject of legalised abortion and "Roe v. Wade." I want to expand a little in this chapter, to give some background knowledge into why this landmark decision was such a devastating blow to the culture, including the very woman at the epicentre.

To begin with, Roe v. Wade was a court case that happened between 1970-1973 that became a landmark decision by the United States Supreme Court on the issue of abortion. **That officially legalized abortion in America.** The Court ruled 7–2 that a right to privacy under the Due Process Clause of the 14th Amendment extended to a woman's decision to have an abortion.

According to Encyclopædia Britannica the facts about this case are as follows: **"Roe v. Wade,** was a legal case in which the U.S. Supreme Court on January 22, 1973, ruled (7–2) that unduly restrictive state regulation of abortion is unconstitutional. In a majority opinion written by Justice Harry A. Blackmun, the court held that a set of Texas statutes criminalizing abortion in most instances violated a woman's constitutional right of privacy, which it found to be implicit in the liberty guarantee of the due process clause of the Fourteenth Amendment ('…nor shall any state deprive any person of life, liberty, or property, without due process of law').

The case began in 1970 when **'Jane Roe' — a fictional name used to protect the identity of the plaintiff, Norma McCorvey** - instituted federal action against Henry Wade, the district attorney of Dallas county, Texas, where Roe resided. The Supreme Court disagreed with Roe's assertion of an absolute right to terminate pregnancy in any way and at any time and attempted to balance a woman's right of privacy with a state's interest in regulating abortion.

In his opinion, Blackmun noted that only a 'compelling state interest' justifies regulations limiting 'fundamental rights' such as privacy and that legislators must therefore draw statutes narrowly 'to express only the legitimate state interests at stake.'

The court then attempted to balance the state's distinct compelling interests in the health of pregnant women and in the potential life of fetuses. It placed the point after which a state's compelling interest in the pregnant woman's health would allow it to regulate abortion 'at approximately the end of the first trimester' of pregnancy.

With regard to the fetus, the court located that point at 'capability of meaningful life outside the mother's womb,' or viability. Repeated challenges since 1973 narrowed the scope of *Roe v. Wade* but did not overturn it."

The article in Britannica concluded with this statement: "In 1998... McCorvey publicly declared her opposition to abortion."[1]

The Feminist Agenda and the Culture Wars of the 1970's

The irony of this infamous case is that Norma McCorvey (aka Jane Roe) did not die as a pro-abortion activist but as a pro-life advocate and a Christian convert.

"McCorvey was just 22 years-old when she stepped into the spotlight as 'Jane Roe' in the historic Roe. v. Wade Supreme Court case of 1973. However, while Roe. v. Wade officially legalized abortion in America, **McCorvey later deeply regretted her role in the case and became a Christian.**

'Back in 1973, I was a very confused twenty-one year old with one child and facing an unplanned pregnancy,' she says in an ad released nearly 10 years ago. 'At the time I fought to obtain a legal abortion, but truth be told, I have three daughters and never had an abortion.'

'Upon knowing God, I realized that my case, which legalized abortion on demand was the biggest mistake of my life,' she adds. 'I think it's safe to say that the entire abortion industry is based on a lie.'

McCorvey didn't want to be remembered as the woman behind the biggest abortion case in America, but as a vocal pro-life activist.

'You read about me in history books, but now I am dedicated to spreading the truth about preserving the dignity of all human life from natural conception to natural death,' she concluded in the ad.

Father Frank Pavone, National Director of Priests for Life, was a close friend to McCorvey and was a key figure in her faith life. 'Norma has been a friend of mine, and of Priests for Life, for more than 20 years,' Father Pavone said in a statement following her death.

'She was victimized and exploited by abortion ideologues when she was a young woman but she came to be genuinely sorry that a decision named for her has **led to the deaths of more than 58 million children.'**

Fr. Pavone also said McCorvey would want pro-life activists to continue the fight for life."[2]

It is well documented that this case happened during the culture wars of the 1970s in America and that Norma McCorvey fell victim to a pair of radical feminist lawyers, Linda Coffee and Sarah Weddington and their feminist agenda.

With no concern for Norma's personal situation they exploited her so that they could drive home a test-case all the way to the Supreme Court, in order to overturn State-level prohibitions on abortion. It is widely recognised that Coffee and Weddington used Norma's vulnerability and made a pawn of her, to advance their campaign of legalizing abortion.

It's important to point out that the trial itself took three years, in which Norma never attended a single session. In the duration, her baby had already been born and given up for adoption, due to her mental and material state. She said that she had been depressed at the time and was referred to the two lawyers in question. Thus their open exploitation of Norma McCorvey deeply contradicted and exposed their disingenuous claims and false *concern* for women in difficult situations.

As the saying goes, "sunlight is the best disinfectant" especially when it comes to corrupt intentions. For more information on the fake feminist agenda you'll have to read my next book.

❖

CHAPTER 19

Gen Z Takeover

To continue, I want to progress onto the subject of Generation Z, (aka iGeneration/iGen, or Centennials), which is probably the most thumping and pulsating generation who have ever lived. I wait with eager expectation to see how this particular cohort develops. I have great expectations. Not because of predictions from analysts, professional number crunchers and satiations. Rather it's a feeling of pure excitement in my belly, whenever I think about Gen Z.

To help establish what Gen Z actually stands for, let me introduce you to nineteen-year-old Patrick Finnegan for some initial perspective:

According to CNNMoney, "Finnegan has established himself as something of a Gen Z expert. He consults for marketing firms like Havas Luxe and is a partner at venture capital fund, Studio.VC. **Gen Z, to be clear, is not the same as Millennial. The group is younger -- born in the late '90s to mid-2000s -- and expected to outgrow Millennials in size and buying power.** Gen Z's buying power is already an estimated $44 billion.

Entrepreneurial and Intergenerational

This young businessman/entrepreneur, Patrick Finnegan, whose new business venture is named: "Gen Z Takeover" is confident of being ahead of the curve. Giving the impression that he holds a firmer grip on reality than the rest of us.

"Brands that used to solely focus on Millennials are just now getting how important Gen Z is, and I can help make that transition."

He's just one example; yet with a massive following on social media, making six figures a year doing consultancy work with businesses in New York, he's already established himself as an "influencer" for his generation.

Take notice that Gen Zers are far more willing to get out of the box and any demographic confines to think bigger and work right across the board.

"Finnegan moved to Manhattan and re-launched his career. Now, at 19, he works with major marketing firms, investors and fund managers to **help them understand younger demographics.**

Since moving to New York City, he's amassed an impressive list of contacts -- including CEOs, billionaires, and prominent angel investors. 'I have a couple dozen people I can call, and say, 'Can you put $50 [thousand]?' Sometimes $1 million, sometimes $2 million,' Finnegan said.

His **ability to network** is a big reason *Studio.VC* founder Liam Lynch hired Finnegan. 'Patrick is a fantastic networker, and he is a quick study on what people are interested in,' said Lynch, who previously built Broadway marketing firm *Key Brand Entertainment*. **'From my experience, there are great benefits to intergenerational teams.'**[1]

The Fact Checking Generation

I think most generations today are learning to become fact-checkers, including my husband's - the Baby Boomers. Yet I concede, that fact checking today has become big business and Gen Zers will excel in this area, like no other.

We can use demographics to help us share the gospel better. However we know that the primary reason for looking at generational cohorts was mainly for marketing purposes, viewing different sections of society in view of their buying power and voting potential.

Nowadays Facebook and Twitter have helped to pin down what's trending at any given moment, with the corporate world continually trying to get inside people's brains, to figure out how best to market their goods to them.

However due to a new culture of fact-checking, big businesses have had to change their tactics and marketing strategies, as their old advertising tricks no longer work. Like all of us, they've had to evolve to keep up.

To reinforce this Robin Koval, co-author of the forthcoming book "Grit to Great," says of Gen Zers that they are **"...a little more practical. They're a little more realistic about life.** They've grown up with uncertainty... There's the expectation that they're going to have to be pretty gritty to make it in the world. **They are entrepreneurial and they are mobile and social natives... They have never known not having a device in their hands... They fact-check everything, so over-the-top claims don't fly."**[2]

The Great Return to Common Sense

So we can see that Gen Zers aren't afraid to be intergenerational. They're not easily threatened by other cohorts and are willing to work together. They're ever pragmatic for their age and there is a good chance that this particular generation will be the ones who finally go full circle. By this I mean, that they might just be the generation that returns to the classic concept of common sense.

Being absorbed for months with several back-to-back (and historical) campaigns, I was feeling the need for a bit of a break from politics. Then I saw a refreshing interview, conducted outdoors in a large crowd, random and spontaneous. In the crowd was a very normal looking 17-year-old young man.

After everyone else had spoken, he calmly gave his point of view. Having been asked the exact same questions as everyone else, his replies were more succinct and on point than everyone else put together. He was in a crowd that did not agree with him, yet his composure was beyond his years. He had something no one else had. Confidence.

It matters little what the interviewer was asking him. What mattered most was, his posture. He was not ashamed of his views. He didn't feel obliged to be politically correct but remained very polite. He looked everyone in the eye and did not feel the need to justify his opinions. He wasn't apologetic and was completely solid and *genuine*.

I think we have become so used to the disingenuous that the genuine shocks us today. It's a PC culture that we've endured for far too long. Political correctness has driven us nuts. And with new terminologies like *micro-aggressions* afflicting us, can we really take much more!

Identifying Authenticity

We've been told what to think and what to say for so long. Yet these confident young kids come out of nowhere and speak clear and precise common sense. I love it. This is why there is so much scope for Gen Z to be a new breed of unequivocal, smart and authentic young people.

Not scripted or over opinionated just calm, grown up, sure of themselves and real. Gen Zers in my eyes have massive potential that will far exceed that of Millennials.

They're basically old souls on young shoulders but may very well be the generation who usher in the return of our Lord. I think that Millennials are over-rated in some respects and under-rated in others. Whereas Gen Zers are uniquely poised to become something very special indeed and I'm honestly excited about them.

❖

CHAPTER 20

So Make Way for Generation Z

The following involves some research that I did concerning this particular demographic. Back in March 2015 an article was written in the New York Times called **"Make Way for Generation Z,"** written by Alexandra Levit. It is lengthy but I like how it transitions from Gen X to Gen Y and ends up with Gen Z. It's a good overview:

"I recall the exact moment the temperature changed in the workplace. It was 2005, and I was speaking to an audience of 100 young professionals. I was relating my experiences building a career as a **Gen Xer (born 1964-79) in a world of traditionalists (born before 1945) and Baby Boomers (born 1946-63).**

Every time I threw out phrases like 'paying your dues' and 'playing the game,' the audience stared at me blankly.

133

This was not the reaction I had come to expect from early twenty-somethings. Usually they took notes on how they could get ahead in corporate America as quickly as possible.

I would soon learn, however, that the Millennial Generation (also known as Generation Y, born after 1980), had come on the scene. **Generally speaking, these guys didn't like my advice about coping with bureaucracy and office politics.**

It seemed to me that some of them didn't want to grow up, but at the same time they felt they deserved to do meaningful work right away. Many were not afraid to speak their minds and made it clear they wanted to change the status quo. **And at 80 million strong, they had the numbers to do it.**

It took 10 years before most organizations identified the Millennials as a talent issue on fire. **By now, the oldest Millennials are 35. They aren't children anymore** — in fact, a majority of them are leaders with decision-making power and direct reports."

Behind the Scenes Curious and Driven

"While executives have been fretting over the Millennials, though, a new generation is growing up behind the scenes — Generation Z (born starting in the mid-90s to the early '00s depending on whom you ask). Within the next three years, Gen Zers will be the college grads in my audiences, and **they are poised to be somewhat different from the Millennials.**

I've now had the opportunity to meet lots of Gen Zers, and here's what I've noticed. **To start, they tend to be independent.** While a 2015 Census Bureau report found that **nearly a third of Millennials are still living with their parents,** Gen Zers are growing up in a healthier economy and appear eager to be cut loose. **They don't wait for their parents to teach them things or tell them how to make decisions.**

As demonstrated by the teenagers attending the recent Generation Z Conference at American University in Washington, **Gen Z is already out in the world, curious and driven,** investigating how to obtain relevant professional experience before college."

Prepared for the Global Environment

"Despite their obvious technology proficiency, Gen Zers seem to prefer in-person to online interaction and are being schooled in emotional intelligence from a young age. Thanks to social media, they are accustomed to engaging with friends all over the world, **so they are well prepared for a global business environment."**

Gen Z and Ethnic Diversity

Alexandra Levit goes on to say, "My 15-year-old next-door neighbour is a quarter Hispanic, a quarter African-American, a quarter Taiwanese, and a quarter white. That's Gen Z — they are often a mix of ethnicities.

Doug Anderson, managing partner of the Washington-based education company 'Bisnow Ventures' organized the

Gen Z conference. He is trying to create a movement around Gen Z with the goal of harnessing the excitement high-school-age Americans have about their careers and helping them explore their options.

At the conference, a few hundred teenagers gathered to take that first step. **The mood was electric.**

Among those who attended was Sejal Makheja, 16, a sophomore who lives in McLean, Va. When she was 14, Sejal founded 'The Elevator Project' an organization that aims to lift people out of poverty through apprenticeship, vocational training and job placement. She said she went to the Gen Z Conference because she wanted to cultivate the skills she'll need to take the 'Elevator Project' to a national scale.

'The young people at the conference want to take an active role in their communities and their futures,' she said. 'It's an upbeat group that's full of passion.'

Anything but Traditional

Sejal signed up for sessions on finance, investing and networking. She says that her parents did not push her to register for the Gen Z event, nor do they help her with her non-profit organization. **'My parents are supportive, and they've had to drive me around, but generally they're pretty hands-off,'** she said. Many Gen Zers intend to go to traditional college, but after that, their lives and careers are likely to be **anything but traditional.**

Even well-known organizations will have to rethink their recruiting practices to attract this group, and now is the time to start. Those who want to take advantage of Gen Z talent in the future need to develop relationships today with teenagers in grades seven through 12. Get into their schools, provide mentorship and education, and put yourself in a position to help shape their career decisions. **They are eager to listen."**

Finally consistent with Patrick Finnegan's ethos for his venture called "Gen Z Takeover," Alexandra finishes by saying, "Filling the talent pipeline has never been so critical now that the United States is facing a skills gap in most industries. Even if you're a small operation, you can still have a Gen Z internship program. **These children are so mature and they learn so fast, they might just be ready to take over by the time they're 22."**[1]

Defining Words

So when trying to comprehend this new and powerful demographic, let's pause for thought, on some of the descriptions assigned to them:

1. Independent and eager to cut lose
2. Curious and driven
3. Technology proficient
4. Mature
5. Fast learners
6. Eager to listen
7. Anything but traditional
8. Well prepared

9. Diverse

10. A mix of ethnicities

11. Prefer in-person to online interaction

12. Have been schooled in emotional intelligence

13. Accustomed to engaging with friends all over the world

14. Prepared for a global business environment

EQ - Emotional Intelligence

EQ (opposed to IQ) is something that Gen Zers are supposed to be better schooled in, than previous generations. For the unschooled however, here is a current definition: "Emotional intelligence (EQ) is the ability to identify, use, understand, and manage your own emotions in positive ways to relieve stress, communicate effectively, empathize with others, overcome challenges and defuse conflict. This ability also allows us to recognize and understand what others are experiencing emotionally. This recognition and understanding is, for the most part, a nonverbal process that informs thinking and influences how well you connect with others.

Emotional intelligence differs from how we think of intellectual ability, in that emotional intelligence is learned — not acquired. This learning can take place at any time in life so the social and emotional skill set, known as emotional intelligence, is something we can all have."[2]

Basically EQ is the capacity to be aware of, control, and express one's emotions along with the ability to handle relationships thoughtfully and sympathetically. Today EQ holds much weight and is considered by some, as equally important as IQ for personal and professional success.

❖

CHAPTER 21

Gen Z - Millennials on Steroids

So life doesn't stop with the Millennials. But to hear some people talking, you would think so. Yet Gen Zers are potentially Millennials on steroids, as this following article by Jeffrey Hayzlett would suggest:

"Lately it seems we've been bombarded from all angles about Millennials. Marketers are tripping over themselves to cater to this **highly influential crowd** and businesses everywhere are looking to hire this **digitally native** crowd for their **tech skills** and **their determination to make a difference** – and not just to the company's bottom line.

Now, we are getting ready for yet another generation – Gen Z (or Centennials) that will be entering the workforce in just a few short years. **Generation Z, born between 1994 and**

2010, are still too young to be a major influence – the oldest of them about to finish college and the youngest barely out of diapers, but once they come of age, their numbers will be far greater than the current Millennial Generation.

When they do join the workforce, what can we expect from them? Will their characteristics resemble Millennials or will they be alien to us? Will they have the same entrepreneurial spirit? How will they affect the workforce?

Millennials gave us Miley Cyrus, Lena Dunham and Mark Zuckerberg – all highly influential in their own way, have helped define a generation described as brash, narcissistic and, to some, entitled. So, what will Gen Z be like?

These are all questions that marketers and brands out there are struggling to define as we speak. However, people shouldn't be so quick to dismiss Gen Z's just yet just because they're young. **According to census data, Gen Zers will outnumber Millennials by nearly one million, putting their numbers at 60 million in the U.S. alone.**

In order to begin to understand what Gen Z can offer, here are a few starting points:

- **They're digital.** While Millennials were considered the first true digital natives and were defined by iPods and MySpace (cue chuckle), **Gen Zers will be the first generation to be fully raised in the smartphone era. They might be defined as the Internet-in-its-pocket generation. Some**

Millennials might remember dial-up, Gen Zers can't remember a time without technology at their fingertips.

- Also, both generations **devour online reviews for everything** – from restaurants, to apps, to places to go, shop and where to go on vacation.

- **View entrepreneurship as a way to success. Entrepreneurship is in a Gen Zers' DNA.** Whereas previous generations were content with working summer jobs at a variety of fast food joints (and nothing wrong with that), these younger generations, would rather create an app that will further revolutionize social media and have a direct impact on people's daily lives.

  They'd rather create their own business just like those who've made it big. In fact, 28% of Gen Zers and Millennials combined said they want to start their own business, according to the third-largest staffing agency in the U.S.

- **Want information instantly, but lose interest just as fast.** Basically, Gen Zers have a rather small attention span and marketers have taken notice of this. In an era of emojis and eight-second Vines, how do marketers get the attention of this generation with a purchasing power of close to $200 billion annually? (source: Mintel) By figuring out ways to communicate in five words and a big picture. Otherwise, they will not reach this generation.

- **Online personas.** While Millennials were quick to jump into the Facebook bandwagon, many on Gen Z prefer to gather at more anonymous social media platforms, such as Secret, Whisper, and SnapChat. **They also prefer the intimacy and immediacy of personalized online shopping; whereas Millennials still prefer to gather at the mall.**

- **Failure might be an option.** No one likes to fail. I think we all get that, but these kids are so young that if at first they don't succeed, rather than wallow in self-pity – like most of us have done, they'll just dust themselves up and try again knowing full well they have the rest of their lives ahead of them; therefore, more opportunities for success. **Basically, they're not afraid to fail. It's a great quality to have."**

What The Rise of Gen Z Means For Brands

So, there's no naivety here. The whole interest in Millennials or Gen Zers all concerns their buying power. It's not their personality that corporates are interested in but the influence they'll have on the economy. Obviously.

Hayzlett continues, "The ease to which Gen Z is able to access technology presents both advantages and challenges for brands that want to reach them. On one hand, **the digital footprint this generation leaves behind is rich and plenty** and companies have the luxury of having all the necessary information to target them with at their fingertips.

As a result, companies know their likes, dislikes, purchasing predilections and everything in between. On the other hand, many companies are at a bit of a loss as to what to do with that information, mainly because of the elusiveness of this new generation, but also because they are so young and will more than likely change their minds as they grow older.

Elusiveness and unpredictability are not things that make business people happy. But try to reach them you must."

Jeffrey Hayzlett continues, **"While their purchasing power is currently slightly lower than their generational counterparts, brands are currently waging war on these teenagers now for their brand loyalty.** They believe the sooner they can lock in that brand loyalty, they'll have a leg up when they come of age and fully enter the workforce. **And since their numbers will be bigger than Millennials, the purchasing power will be greater as well.**

In order to reach this generation, brands need to learn how to use the technology Gen Zers use. It's a matter of **'adapt, change or die.'** This is a common theme with me. It's the right way to approach business, regardless of which generation you're trying to cater to. **If you're stuck with ideas from the past, you'll never move forward. It's that simple.**

Brands also need to stay ahead of any potential negative comments and opinions that customers express online — **always!** Companies need to invest in more resources towards social media management in order to build awareness and increase exposure for their brands.

It wouldn't hurt to hire a brand ambassador that spoke directly to that audience and helped create a conversation between the brands and the customer. Also, if the ultimate goal is to win the hearts and minds of Gen Z, **retailers must offer cool tools that put these teens and tweens in charge of the development process and must also counter their impatient tendencies by creating something that's quick and to the point.**

As an entrepreneur myself, I must let go of my preconceived notions about this younger generation if I'm to move forward. **I'll be the first to admit, I probably don't have much in common with Millennials, much less Gen Zers; however, if I'm to thrive in business,** I must adapt to the ever-changing business world, adopt the latest gadgets and make it my business to know what I don't know.

You need to make it your business as well! **If the saying is true, that Gen Zers are 'Millennials on steroids,' we're in for a very interesting ride in the not-so distant future."**[1]

❖

CHAPTER 22

Influencers, Disrupters and the Mavericks

Going back to the ambitions of young Mr Finnegan, who described himself as an "influencer" and "disruptor," saying he wanted to **disrupt the establishment because it needs to be disrupted,"** exposes that even the youngest generation is feeling the anti-establishment vibe that's sweeping the globe.

It's a mood that's on the surge and is not limited to one particular generation or demographic. It's being felt and expressed across all age barriers. Perhaps we can call it intergenerational-populism!

It's hard not to mention recent events, as they have been so dominant in the news. Yet I mention them again because

I want to make a point. As much as I like Gen Z and the Millennials, they are by no means unique.

When it comes to being influencers and disrupters of the status quo; while they may have a drive for it, they are a little late on the scene! People have been disrupting the status quo for generations and you don't have to be young or in a certain age bracket to be an influencer or disrupter.

At the time of writing this book, "recent events" once again refers predominantly to Brexit and the Trump election victory. UKIP's leader Nigel Farage and the American billionaire-businessman-turned-politician have emerged as unpredictable voices in modern politics that both tapped into the same tide of discontent, that's rocking the boat everywhere.

This includes the ever-changing political climate of the European Union, especially in France and the Netherlands, that both represent their own brand of anti-establishment-populism, with the likes of Marine Le Pen and Dutch politician Geert Wilders. Who, it might be worth pointing out - with a little jest – all possess, along with Boris Johnson and Donald Trump, curious amounts of blonde hair. (Pure coincidence!)

More seriously though, the *establishment* and *mainstream media* have pushed back rather hard against all such changes in tide, by mocking not only these *messengers* but also by ridiculing their base, (those who vote for them).

This rise of populism is not unique to them of course, but also proceeds through the ranks of Greece and Italy, and many other countries who are now turning their collective backs, on *elites* for bullying, corruption and decades of unfair policies that don't work or translate into reality for people on the streets.

No longer is it the day of identity politics, but the forgotten man and woman who sit around their kitchen tables, worrying how to make ends meet and NOT about what *celebrities* think about them, from their walled villas with bank accounts full of money!

It's now the day, for the regular man and woman to rise up and have their voices heard and their needs met with real solutions. To have their fears addressed and desire for safety, heard in the halls of power, by representatives doing their job in government and not just posturing.

Politicians who'll speak for them in places of influence and not just speak into an echo chamber and get nothing done; who'll do more than just lobby for special interest groups and speak out for regular families; the same people who demand borders and safer limits on immigration in the countries they live in the same as they want doors on the houses they live in.

Is demanding security and safety for one's family bigoted, racist or prejudiced? Would you not vet people coming through your own front door, to ensure that you're not inviting paedophiles into the same living space as your own children? Don't we owe that to them, to keep them sheltered and protected? Isn't it part of their "human rights" to expect that from their own parents?

Is common sense really becoming a thing of the past? Are we trading common sense and logic with whimsical and dangerous liberal philosophies that don't produce any rational solutions?

The Rise of the Mavericks

However it's those who are unorthodox, who possess enough backbone to stand up to big government, that are helping voice this collective plea for systemic change. Included in this unlikely band of mavericks and change agents is former Mayor of London, Mr Boris Johnson.

Heavily criticized and often credited for Brexit, Mr Johnson really just helped many to articulate their already existing and long standing concerns and sentiments about Europe, such as: immigration, sovereignty and freedom from the tyranny of unelected bureaucrats in Brussels.

Although eccentric (Boris also having unusual hair) no one would dispute his intellectual prowess and successful tenure as Mayor, notwithstanding his promotion to foreign secretary in Theresa May's cabinet.

We have to face it, that the prevailing *anti-establishment-mood* of recent years is not abating but growing, against all efforts to slow it down. It's influencing the Baby Boomers right down to the Gen Zers and is not limited, as traditionally thought, to the lower classes. Everyone's feeling it!

So what's happening? People are tired of fake news and fake democracy; told they have a free vote but then told how to vote! People of all generations are rising up and demanding authentic change.

What's the point to all of this? We can tap into this mood for the *authentic* by offering "the Christ solution" as the "only solution."

What Comes Next after Gen Z?

What comes after Generation Z? Will this alphabetic system start again from scratch or will it become obsolete and irrelevant – as some already suggest that it is?

According to Fortune, "Z is the end of the alphabet, but it may be the end of the line for this naming game for other reasons. First, for people to constitute a generation, they must experience the same things. 'We in the media and marketing are still grouping people in *15-20 year cohorts,'* says Alexandra Levit. **'Increasingly, it isn't making any sense.'** Technology is changing rapidly, and there will come a moment when it reaches, 'such an advanced point that we can't even imagine what our lives will be like,' Levit concludes."[1]

How can we imagine what our children's lives will be like in the future? There will be driverless cars and pizza delivered by drones! What will it be like growing up in this kind of environment?

Plus the governments of the world are moving more and more towards a one-world order type of governing, with no borders, no boundaries and no freedom! People talk of freedom but there is no freedom. The more dominant a role that government plays, with such manipulating façades and smokescreens as human rights, environmental issues and political correctness, the more that *offenses* will increase, while our ability to defend our rights and freedoms will decrease.

I agree with the author of, Courage to do Nothing, when he says, "Socialism is inherently flawed, but instead of allowing the free market to function, our politicians employ **socialism concealed as compassion. Our cultural elites in Washington, Academia, Media, and Hollywood have built a modern Tower of Babel based on progressive fantasies...**

Socialism is but one pillar in this faulty tower, but it is the pillar du jour and America's future if we don't restore the traditional Christian values and limited government our nation was built upon **...ignored by the cultural elites..."**[2]

The same is true universally. Not just in America, of course. Progressive ideas are proliferating society through social and cultural osmosis and are being met with little if any resistance, as my husband says below:

> **"The church, to a large extent, is allowing these governments to develop this way, because the body of Christ has not been the voice or influencing power in the world that it should have been."**
> - Dr Alan Pateman

❖

CHAPTER 23

Its True Meaning -
The Separation of Church and State

This brings me to a very important issue, which involves a complex subject called "the separation of church and state," which contrary to popular opinion, was originally intended **to stop government meddling in church affairs, not the other way around.**

The church was always meant to be a voice in the world. It was never designed solely to preach to the choir! The body of Christ was always meant to be a commanding influence on politics, for the better and not the worse. So, as you will see, the systematic *muting* of the church, in the affairs of government, has come about due to some rather calculating and *liberal* twisting of the law.

So let's explore this a little, as it has become such a fundamental issue spanning the globe, and has helped shape world affairs, not solely in the United States.

Helping to lend some much needed clarity into the complexities of this matter, my research took me, amongst other things, to an article written in Forbes Business Magazine. The author of which is called Bill Flax, who describes himself as, "a Christian, patriot and defender of liberty."

However his article below, was written back in 2011, which in my humble opinion was an excellent piece of writing and considering recent political developments worldwide, couldn't be more relevant. It's an insightful and succinct historical overview and reads as follows:

Local Autonomy

"Our nation was predicated on unalienable rights with governance through family, church and community, each rightfully sovereign within its sphere. Human dignity, legal equality and personal freedom reflect biblical values imparted on Western Civilization, **which retains these values in secular form while expunging their Author from public discourse.**

Americans are frequently reminded of what the revisionists deem our greatest achievement: **'Separation of Church and State.'** Crosses are ripped down in parks. Prayer has been banished from schools and the ACLU rampages to remove 'under God' from the Pledge of Allegiance. **Moreover, 'Separation of Church and State' is nowhere**

found in the Constitution or any other founding legislation. Our forefathers would never countenance the restrictions on religion exacted today.

The phrase 'separation of church and state,' was initially coined by Baptists striving for religious toleration in Virginia, whose official state religion was then Anglican (Episcopalian). Baptists thought government limitations against religion illegitimate. James Madison and Thomas Jefferson championed their cause.

The preamble in Act Establishing Religious Freedom in Virginia (1786), affirms that 'the Author of our religion gave us our *free will*.' And that He 'chose not to propagate it by coercions.' **This legislation certainly did not diminish religious influence on government for it also provided stiff penalties for conducting business on the Sabbath.**

Nor did the Constitution inhibit public displays of faith. At ratification, a majority of the thirteen several and sovereign states maintained official religions. The early Republic welcomed public worship. Church services were held in the U.S. Capitol and Treasury buildings every Sunday. The imagery in many federal buildings remains unmistakably biblical.

The day after the First Amendment's passage, Congress proclaimed a national day of prayer and thanksgiving. The inaugural Congress was largely comprised by those who drafted the Constitution. It reflects incredible arrogance to reconfigure the Bill of Rights into prohibiting religious displays on public grounds. Hanging the Ten Commandments on the wall of a county courthouse no more mandates religion than judges displaying the banner of their favorite sports team somehow equates to Congress establishing that team as preeminent.

Our forefathers never sought to evict the church from society. They recognized that the several states did not share uniform values. We lived and worshipped differently. The framers were a diverse bunch with wildly divergent opinions on many issues, but **eliminating the very foundations of America's heritage would have horrified them. On few issues was there more unanimity.**

Where the French Revolution and its official policy of 'De-Christianization' quickly devolved into bloodshed and oppression, here freedom flourished. Our independence was seen as the culmination of a march toward liberty, not a rejection of America's historical cultural moorings. Our forbears embraced tradition and left local autonomy largely intact.

Schools, courts and the public square were often overtly Christian and had been since their colonial beginnings. Few Americans would have tolerated a coercive central government infringing on their rights to post religious symbols on local schools, courts or anywhere else.

Americans built society from the ground up. Many had fled oppression. The colonies instituted local self-government indigenously to confirm the rights resident in their persons and property. Few would have willingly been dispossessed by Washington of the very freedoms, which they had just secured from London.

Here men could and did rise as their efforts merited. Commoners were unshackled from feudal paralysis and freed to find God individually. Both the economy and church thrived. **Alexis de Tocqueville observed that Americans intertwined individual liberty with vibrant faith. 'It is impossible to make them conceive the one without the other.'**

Even non-Christian founders thought religion essential. None would have wished to upend the very basis for education, law or culture. The Northwest Ordinance of 1787 states: **'Religion, morality, and knowledge, being necessary to good government and the happiness of mankind, schools and the means of education shall forever be encouraged.'**

Freedom of Conscience

Americans understood freedom without morality quickly devolves into debauchery. Whether from sincere faith, or, prudence instilling an honest, law-abiding, responsible and hardworking populace, all esteemed biblical morality as the bedrock of self government. **George Washington believed, 'Religion and morality are indispensible supports' for 'it is impossible to rightly govern the world without God and the bible.'**

The phrase 'separation between church and state' was reintroduced by former Klansman Hugo Black, historically one of our most liberal Supreme Court judges. In the 1947

Everson v. Board of Education, Justice Black invoked Thomas Jefferson stating, 'The First Amendment has erected 'a wall of separation between church and state.' ...that wall must be kept high and impregnable.'

Thomas Jefferson thought differently. The Danbury Baptists wrote to him congratulating his election and objecting to the First Amendment. **They thought it implied government dispensed what was not government's to give. Jefferson agreed.**

His reply clearly applied 'separation of church and state' to the establishment and not to the free exercise of religion. As he expressed, what communities did and how they worshipped were not federal affairs. Jefferson later said the central government was **'interdicted from intermeddling with religious institutions.'** Such were state matters.

Freedom of religion was partly moral – protecting our most cherished liberty – and partly pragmatic. Religious animosity tears society asunder, particularly when church is affixed to government. With freedom of conscience assured, conflict becomes less likely. **The First Amendment was an insightful compromise between church and state, federal and local authorities. The framers desired to avoid the controversies, which engulfed Europe.**

As James Madison warned in Federalist 10, 'The latent causes of faction are thus sown in the nature of man; ... A zeal for different opinions concerning religion, concerning government, and many other points, ... ambitiously contending for pre-eminence and power ... divided mankind into parties, inflamed them with mutual animosity, and **rendered them much more disposed to vex and oppress each other than to cooperate for their common good.'**

Thus the Constitution decreed that Washington had no occasion or authority to interject itself into matters as obviously local as doctrines of faith. Congress was not empowered to establish a church because the framers feared that concentrated power, whether favored religions, standing armies, banking monopolies, or an overarching federal government, invited tyranny.

Church and state were distinct in that the Federal Government could not elevate one denomination over others. Nor could government and its flawed inhabitants usurp divine authority by harnessing politics to the church. Faith is no civil contract, but a personal matter not to be profaned by politics.

State controlled churches frequently exploited this latent power for evil. The **Spanish Inquisition didn't originate in the Vatican, but the Castilian court.** It was not of the church, but the king. **By Philip II, Spain had the makings of the first police state infused with the ill-gotten moral authority of a tyrannical clergy.**

Bill of Rights

Much of our Bill of Rights was meant to prevent dictatorships such as Cromwell's, which married church and state in such manner as to mar many of the freedoms our forefathers sought to enshrine.

The framers witnessed the incessant wars of the mother continent and understood official churches and centralized power fomented abuses. Having two or three competing factions spurred struggles between the parties to secure power, but divesting authority to innumerable smaller jurisdictions without the prospect of any gaining control promoted peaceful freedom.

Episcopalians in Virginia would live amicably next to Catholics in Maryland, Quakers in Pennsylvania or Baptists in their midst. None saw cause for contention because there was no threat that others would gain dominion over them or any prospect that they might gain such dominion themselves. Rivalry was unnecessary because **'Congress shall make no law respecting an establishment of religion.'**

Establishment has been redefined. Limitations on government have been altered into restrictions on religious expression, which clearly violates the amendment's next clause: **'prohibiting the free exercise thereof'** and third clause **'abridging the freedom of speech.'**

Meanwhile, Washington publicly imposes politically correct secular religions like worshiping diversity or the environment.

Are our rights inalienable or contrivances from courts? Is government still limited or its power undefined? Is the state answerable to the people or are we but subjects? Do our rights descend from God or derive from man? America must decide."[1]

I have purposely included the entirety of this article, so as not to take anything away from it. As it is such a rich explanation concerning the factually correct intention and original context for "the separation of church and state," that many have a selective blindness towards today!

The Global Attempt of De-Christianization

Instead, nowadays we see *everything* being re-interpreted through the lens of political correctness, which often times, is not just extremely *liberal* but also *diabolically* motivated and poses a great threat to our modern society.

His short mention of the **French Revolution and its official policy of "De-Christianization,"** could describe much of what's going on in most countries today. And how such philosophy prevents countries from thriving and instead they, "quickly devolve into bloodshed and oppression..." Again, aptly describing events as they stand now. Where riots and violent protests are becoming more commonplace.

Quite simply, whether it's here in Europe or in America, there is an ongoing attempt right across the western world, involving nefarious deep-state and unelected elites and bureaucrats who want to De-Christianize the modern world, as we know it. They call this democracy, while monitoring, influencing, manipulating and even dictating our every move!

Millennials are coming of age in a crucial time in history, that many are considering the beginning of the new cold war. While others think it never ended!

As for Gen Zers, they are set to live out their formative years, in a whole new era. An era perhaps that will see an end to all such demographic cycles and help usher in the next phase - the Second Coming, our Lord's return. **We owe it to them, to get them ready.**

CHAPTER 24

Modern Populism v. The Babylonian System

The Babylonian system represents the elite establishment and modern populism represents a transition of power back to the people - as it should be. Like Lincoln's famous Gettysburg Address that said, "Government of the people, by the people, for the people, shall not perish from the Earth." Opposed to government overreach, police states and cronyism.

The establishment elite versus the people, is like the Babylonian system versus the *movement* of the people, where they rise up and fact check what they are being told by the media and making their own minds up.

In his teaching Dr Alan Pateman says, **"When God is allowed to move it will *delay* the Babylonian system."**

Just briefly let me say something on immigration – it's a hot-blooded issue with many sides – and we must remember that places like America are almost entirely made up of immigrants. Basically, according to scripture we aught to welcome foreign aliens. However nowhere does scripture instruct that we welcome foreign terrorists (wink!)

Let's see directly what scripture says on this very inflammatory issue:

> *Don't take advantage of any stranger who lives in your land.* **You must treat the outsider as one of your native-born people—as a full citizen—and you are to love him in the same way you love yourself;** *for* **remember,** *you were once strangers living in Egypt. I am the Eternal One, your God.*
> *(Leviticus 19:34 VOICE)*

> *He enforces His justice for the powerless, such as orphans and widows, and* **He loves foreigners, making sure they have food and clothing. You must love those foreigners** *living with you* **in the same way.** *Remember how you were foreigners in the land of Egypt!*
> *(Deuteronomy 10:18-19 VOICE)*

> *He executes justice for the orphan and the widow, and* **shows His love for the stranger (resident alien, foreigner)** *by giving him food and clothing. Therefore, show your love for the stranger, for you were strangers in the land of Egypt (AMP).*

It's imperative we use the New Testament in this context also: "There is neither Greek nor Jew, circumcision nor uncircumcision, Barbarian, Scythian, bond nor free: but **Christ is all, and in all. Put on therefore, as the elect of God, holy and beloved, bowels of mercies, kindness..."** (Colossians 3:10-13 KJV)

However vetting *is* required. Vetting is not unkind or unmerciful. It enables the watchmen on the walls to enforce the correct rule of law, which benefits everyone. The alternative is anarchy and chaos, and scripture is equally clear about that: **"For God is not the author of confusion, but of peace..."** (1 Corinthians 14:33 KJV)

Merkel admits Open Door Policy was a Mistake

Boundaries do exist for healthy reasons, in addition scripture also talks about honouring and protecting ancient boundaries: "Do not move the ancient landmark [at the boundary of the property] which your fathers have set" (Proverbs 22:28 AMP).

"You shall not move your neighbour's boundary mark, which the forefathers [who first divided the territory] have set, in the land which you will inherit in the land which the Lord your God is giving you to possess" (Deuteronomy 19:14 AMP).

So we do need to have borders and we do need to respect and protect them rigorously and righteously, while treating the people inside them, fairly and justly. This subject requires much more ink and paper, but I don't want to labour the point anymore right here.

An open border without proper vetting is not a very smart concept. Something that Germany has found out, the hard way. And with Germany's horrible past still vividly in history's rear-view-mirror, it's believed that this motivated Angela Merkel to open the German borders to over one million refugees. I guess robust vetting would have created too much of a paper trail!

One recent article wrote: **"Merkel admits her 'Open Door' migrant policy was a mistake:** One year after suspending European Union (EU) rules and inviting 'no upper limit' of migrants to Germany, Angela Merkel has admitted she made mistakes. **'We didn't embrace the problem in an appropriate way. That goes as well for *protecting the external border of the Schengen area,'* the German Chancellor said in an interview, finally admitting some responsibility for the migrant crisis."[1]

"An appeaser is one who feeds a crocodile, hoping it will eat him last."

- Winston Churchill

Tolerance of Intolerance is Suicide

There are consequences. Now jihadi-migrants are biting the very hand that feeds them and they are executing their original purpose for "slipping in with the refugees," and that is to extend the Islamic Caliphate, Sharia Law and the creation of apocalyptic fear and havoc in Europe. Let's never be naïve when it comes to Islamic extremism. We can talk all day about how, "not all Muslims are extremists" and we can all agree about that. Sure, not all Muslims are fanatical or murderous.

The point being made here is this: that individuals who've entered Europe, (specifically Germany), as undercover jihadi-soldiers posing as refugees, do not have split loyalties. They are here in Europe to do the bidding of ISIS. Ready to die for the cause.

Just like the kamikaze bombers of Pearl Harbour. It's an honour for these "Islamic fighters" (including an honour for their families), if they die as martyrs. It's a death cult that is difficult for the West to understand or combat. Who is able to stop people who are determined to die - who believe it's better to die than to live - who believe that rewards are waiting for them, for killing as many infidels as possible. Whose families get financially compensated and sweets are handed out in their memory?

It's widely documented that, "The Palestinian Authority spends roughly 10 percent of its annual budget paying terrorists who attack Israelis and supporting their families, according to expert testimony to congressional lawmakers... **'We welcome every drop of blood spilled in Jerusalem. This is pure blood, clean blood, blood on its way to Allah,'** Palestinian President Mahmoud Abbas stated last September on Palestinian television. **'With the help of Allah, every martyr will be in heaven, and every wounded will get his reward.'"**[2]

While discussing the complexities of modern terrorism with Fox anchor, Tucker Carlson, terror expert Sebastian Gorka DrG emphatically stated, **"Tolerance of intolerance is suicide!"**

The Modern Day Trojan Horse

What Western government can counter or hope to resolve this type of ideology? Yet tighter border controls and migrant vetting programs can go a long way in reducing – but not eradicating – the threats.

My own formative years were influenced by nightly reports on the news about the latest killings of the I.R.A movement and the apprehension that hung in the air as a result.

More terrifying is the use of soft targets and human shields, which is something that the Islamic State terrorists are seemingly only too willing to do. As has been reported over and over again.

Let's be clear, aliens and genuine asylum seekers are welcome, but they must be properly vetted. For those escaping persecution, there must be clemency. But let me point out, that Christians are suffering persecution around the globe yet no one in the mainstream media is giving it any oxygen at all. It's receiving very little focus. Persecuted Muslims are receiving lots of help that persecuted Christians are not receiving. Why is that? I guess it's not so politically correct.

Finally, we must remember that fake asylum seekers represent a modern day Trojan horse that's not *waiting* to happen, but is *already* happening. It's a strategy of subversion, to create religious and political destabilization.

Although this book is not dedicated to this subject, it pains me to leave it out, as every society is being infiltrated and influenced by this migrant crisis. Elections have been won and lost on this issue alone. So it's not something we can politely brush under an ethical or moral carpet because it's uncomfortable or inconvenient to talk about.

❖

CHAPTER 25

The Rise of the
Modern Populist "Movements"

You may ask: "Why all this political interest?" The simple answer must be: because people's lives are involved. During my bible school days I went knocking door-to-door, as part of an evangelism program in my church. When an aggressive gentleman asked me about the previous evening's news.

When I was unable to comment, the door was abruptly slammed in my face, and I was sternly rebuked for not living in the "real world." The experience was life changing. Ignorance is *not* bliss. We must understand the world that we live in, because we are not ostriches with our heads in the religious sandpit.

People from every demographic cohort are being influenced by radical and very liberal ideas and we must have some perspective and perception about what's going on. Our discernment must reach beyond the church walls to see how God is moving in every arena - as He so loves *this* world.

Below I have briefly attempted to list a very small number of modern populist "movements" (notice the emphasis on *movement* rather than party) that exist today. Yet the few that I do mention are having a mounting and substantial influence on today's politics. Their ideologies and policies come from both the Right and the Left of the political paradigm, even though they claim to be influenced by neither. Either way, all brands of populism are having their effect on society today.

Italy - Europe

M5S - The Five Star Movement - Italy (leans to the political Left):

M5S is a political party in Italy that was started in 2009, by popular comedian and blogger Beppe Grillo and web strategist Gianroberto Casaleggio.

Once again "movement" is the operative word, as M5S openly prefers being considered a *movement* opposed to a political *party*. Not unlike various other movements.

Movimento 5 Stelle (M5S), is considered populist, anti-establishment, environmentalist, anti-globalist and Eurosceptic. Grillo himself referred to his movement as "populist" but categorically doesn't want to be included in the traditional left-right political paradigm.

The 5 Stars represent the five key issues of the movement:

1. Public water
2. Sustainable transport
3. Sustainable development
4. Right to Internet access
5. Environmentalism

First Female Mayor of Rome

In 2016 M5S's Virginia Raggi was elected as the first female Mayor of Rome, at the age of 38, which was a monumental move and who subsequently cancelled Rome's Olympic bid for 2024.

The movement also advocates E-democracy, direct democracy, the principle of zero-cost politics, de-growth and non-violence. In foreign policy, the M5S have condemned military interventions of the West in the Greater Middle East (Afghanistan, Iraq, Libya) as well as any notion of American intervention in Syria.

In the European Parliament the M5S is part of the "Europe of Freedom and Direct Democracy" (EFDD) group, along with the "UK Independence Party" (UKIP).[1]

England

UKIP - The UK Independence Party – (leans to the political Right):

UKIP has been described by many as a right-wing populist party and seen as being radically Right wing and

Eurosceptic. But they don't necessarily agree with this description.

According to a recent article in The Telegraph, MEP Steven Woolfe, UKIP's migration spokesman said, **"UKIP isn't Left-wing or Right-wing. It's just sensible."** Saying that, "The old Left-Right spectrum has no place in today's politics, where leaving the EU is the most radical policy proposed by any party."

Let me reiterate that my thoughts here aren't aligned with one particular political ideology or another. What I am doing is viewing the entire political spectrum as a whole, (by using current examples) and seeing that once very "contrasting" views are not so "contrasting" anymore. **The Right is arguably morphing into the Left and vice-versa. It's increasingly evident that the usual Right and Left wing paradigm is becoming irrelevant.**

With common-sense politics taking more of a lead, people are tiring of the establishment, who promise, but don't deliver. People are demanding authenticity from their representatives, regardless of their race, age or gender. It no longer matters, so long as their ideas are based on common sense and that they are not "bought or sold" by the highest bidder such as unions, special interest groups, lobbyists and big donors.

Such representatives must be natural leaders, able to unite, yet tough enough to get things done. Not play softly-softly with everyone singing *Kum-ba-ya* but focusing on the true transference of power, back to the people, with elected representatives who will serve the peoples' best interests.

Modern Populism - Neither Left or Right

Donald Trump came on the scene, unpredictable, hot blooded and unconventional. Once democrat turned republican – who could distinguish if he was really Right, Left or Centre of the political spectrum?

He baffled everyone. He went from being the ultimate-insider (part of the elite), to being the impassioned common-sense and no-nonsense candidate. Not everyone was convinced, because Trump had morphed. Was it genuine? After all he was not a natural born Politician, what could he possibly know? Yet his tenacious, pragmatic, hard-nosed and can-do businessman's approach pulled it off.

His move from being a pro-abortion Democrat to being a pro-life Republican, was down to personal conviction and in his own words he was, "the ultimate insider," who saw his country "losing all the time - instead of winning."

He saw that the old way of doing things in Washington wasn't working. The status quo and the establishment were corrupt and it was time to disrupt.

The point of the matter again is this; when does investing in wages, jobs, safety and the military, or infrastructure, clean air and water make a person Right-wing or simply doing the Right-thing?

Steven Woolfe highlights this by saying: "The terms 'Left' and 'Right' date back to the French national assembly during the revolution. The French elitists, the rich and the conservatives didn't want change - in fact, they refused to embrace a New France - whereas we saw the Left were seen as the radicals, who proposed and wanted real change."

How things have flipped! By this estimation, the likes of UKIP and Trump would be considered Left while their opponents still consider them Right-wing extremist. This means the whole paradigm has been successfully disrupted and the new has emerged.

It's not Right-Wing it's just the Right-Thing!

Referring back to British politics he goes on to say: "Surely, going off this spectrum, the Liberal Democrats, Labour and the Conservatives would all be firmly on the Right, whereas UKIP would be on the Left? We are after all the only party proposing real change by leaving the European Union.

In practice, because UKIP is not fixated by political ideologies, **these terms are now superfluous for use in sensible UK political debate.** Which is why they have ended up in the gutter, used by... reactionary street thugs like those who tried to inflict violence upon... those they call, 'right-wing scum.'"

Similar to special-interest-groups in America, he goes on to state, "UKIP do not have to kowtow to the outside bodies like unions or corporate sponsors which traditionally anchor political parties on the left or right. We debate those issues that may compromise our principles even though the outcome may be detrimental to our party – UKIP's discussions and the outcome over so-called short money is a case in point.

We are a democratic party that believes in ideas - ideas which are likely to be best for the people of this country, and which will lower the cost of living and increase real wages. That's not Left or Right; it's just UKIP."

Mr Woolfe concludes, "We have been called 'Left-wing' by the Tories time and time again for wanting to scrap means testing for the most vulnerable in society. Meanwhile, Labour call us 'more Tory than the Tories' - code for 'Right-wing' - for wanting such things as well-financed armed forces.

Since when has supporting our armed forces been a Right-wing idea? Supporting our forces is common sense. They put their lives on the line for us, it's only right we support people while they're part of our armed forces and make sure that support is continued when they leave. **It's not Right-wing; it's just the right thing to do."**[2]

❖

CHAPTER 26

The Rise of the Modern Populist "Movements" Part 2

So there you have it. Controversial as they may be, such movements exist. Love them or loathe them, these disrupters are noticeably not Millennials! Although Millennials are involved in these *movements,* the media don't want us to focus on that. But not all Millennials are fodder for the mainstream media, or naïve sheep who just follow.

Instead many of them are educated and have their own minds made up and want to be part of the solution. Time will reveal the true extent of Millennial involvement during the Brexit (including other political upsets internationally). I believe many are going to be shocked.

Nevertheless more disruptions are fast approaching on the political horizon, with various referendums and general elections taking place in different countries across the globe. It's an uprising. People want to be heard. They want a voice. They don't want to feel forgotten or ignored. They feel that the best way to protest is by not voting the way that the media and elite establishment want them to!

Modern Populism

The term populism refers to political groups, which ideologically contrast "the people," against an elite or group of "menacing others" whom the populists claim terrorize or bully the sovereignty of "the people." Central to their populism is its defence of democracy and its claim to represent the true democratic will of the people.

UKIP is just one example of a wider rise in the prominence of Right-wing populist groups across the Western world, and comparisons have been drawn between UKIP and the likes of the Tea Party movement in the United States and the True Finns in Finland.

The Tea Party Movement USA:

Briefly the Tea Party movement is an American political movement known for its conservative positions and its role in the Republican Party. According to various sources, "The movement's name refers to the Boston Tea Party of December 16, 1773, a watershed moment in the start of the American Revolution." And the movement, amongst other things, has opposed government-sponsored universal healthcare and has been described as a mixture of libertarian, populist and conservative activism.

The Rise of the Modern Populist

Millennials are involved. As I've already said, not all Millennials are created equal, this meaning that not all are discerning or even care less. But I'd say most still hate to be patronised and it's hard to fool them. Plus it's become abundantly clear in recent times, that many don't care so much whether it's a man, woman or African American in the White House. What they care about most is authentic change. Not just façades that represent the same old hamster-wheel of corruption and status quo. Authentic, is what they want but politicians and the old political paradigms no longer represent that.

While there is always an exception to every rule, I think that most conventionally accepted "rules" are continually being turned on their faces. Even the newest ones! Millennials for example are considered more tech-savvy yet this doesn't automatically mean that they are all as open to change as we are led to believe. And the Boomers aren't as tech-illiterate as we are always led to believe either. They detest the over-polished, disingenuous career politicians, just as much.

There are many of us, who are not willing to spend the rest of our lives, balancing on a politically-correct-type-rope, regardless of our demographic age. We'd rather make a solid stand instead, one way or the other and politicians, like chameleons, are becoming more and more of an isolated breed.

According to The Business Dictionary, Populism is defined as follows:

"In general, ideology or political movement that mobilizes the population (often, but not always, the lower classes) against an institution or government, usually in the defence of the underdog or the wronged. **Whether of left, right, or middle political persuasion, it seeks to unite the incorrupt and the unsophisticated (the 'little man') against the corrupt dominant elites (usually the orthodox politicians) and their camp followers (usually the rich and the intellectuals).**

It is guided by the belief that political and social goals are best achieved by the direct actions of the masses. Although it comes into being where mainstream political institutions fail to deliver, there is no identifiable economic or social set of conditions that give rise to it, and it is **not confined to any particular social class.**"[1]

Needless to say, there is a groundswell of individuals who are breaking the mould and thinking outside their cultural box. There are *"movements"* that are *on-the-move*. Governments know that *thinking* can be dangerous, especially when people start thinking for themselves.

Such people tend to gather themselves together into groups and begin to organize and seek out a leader who'll be their voice. One thing's for certain, normal paradigms have forever shifted and the usual global political and religious landscapes will eventually become unrecognisable.

❖

CHAPTER 27

What is Globalization?

Obviously certain aspects of life have gone viral. The term global-village for example, used to be used far more often than it is now. But the saturation of Internet usage has connected people globally in a way that was not possible before.

We discussed IT in other chapters, because information technology plays a large role in globalization today. To break it down, globalization involves international integration, especially where worldviews become interchangeable along with products, ideas, and other aspects of culture. Especially major advancements in transportation and communication (Internet and smart phones).

According to some, large-scale globalization only started back in the 1820s but by the late 19th and 20th centuries the connectivity of the world's economies and cultures grew most rapidly.

It could be said today, that globalization is mainly influenced by: trade (transactions and investment), migration (the movement of people), and the distribution of knowledge. **More specifically: economic globalization, cultural globalization and political globalization.**

Globalization is not something that can be stopped. But as we have witnessed with Brexit and other upsets, not everyone wants to lose autonomy (the ability to self-govern or self-rule) or sovereignty (independence). However for others the one-world-order that they've been so badly craving (with its unique currency and religion), couldn't come fast enough.

So much is happening, adapting and changing that it's hard to keep up. And at the time of writing this book, the world still has not come to terms with the election of Donald Trump or that people like Marine Le Pen were genuinely considered a credible candidate, in France! Such sweeping changes would have been unthinkable just a decade ago.

People like Lance Wallnau, one of the early Trump supporters, wrote a book called, "God's Chaos Candidate," likening Donald Trump as a modern day biblical King Cyrus. Who was a secular leader but anointed by God for reformation.

Yet Lance Wallnau also talks much about Millennials. But there are two kinds, secular and non-secular. Believing

Millennials will be part of the reformation but secular Millennials are showing that they readily favour socialism - vast contrast! It's not something that they have experienced in their lifetime and so they are visiting this for the first time. Like vinyl records, a bad comparison perhaps, but it's new to them.

The danger is that because of their lack of experience, they have no way of weighing up the consequences (just look at Venezuela). This bleeds into my narrative, that the last generation has an obligation to instruct the younger. Otherwise they are going to vote on issues that they have no previous experience about. At worst they will repeat the mistakes of the last generation or at best re-invent the wheel every 15/20 years!

Believing v. Secular Millennials

In May 2016 Christianity Today said, **"Turns out, young Christians may be the most engaged bible readers in generations. Practicing Christian Millennials are bucking a trend.** Overall, this generation is less likely to read or trust the bible than any other. More than half (55%) are "bible-neutral" or "bible-skeptical," compared to 45 percent of teens, 51 percent of Gen Xers, 40 percent of Boomers, and 40 percent of elders.

Yet Christian youth who go to church and care about their faith may know the bible better than older Christians. **Practicing Millennials are more likely to believe the bible came from God and read it multiple times a week than any other generation (87%)..."**

They go onto say, "The rise of technology may be aiding Millennials in staying connected to their bibles. Over the last 6 years, the number of those reading the bible online has soared, up from 37 percent of all adults in 2011 to 49 percent in 2016.

Those who used their phones to search for verses or content more than doubled, from 18 percent to 43 percent. Listening to audio versions of the bible (up from 28% to 35%) and listening to bible teaching on podcasts (24% to 37%) also jumped dramatically.

The growing popularity of digital technologies represents an enormous opportunity for those who seek to increase bible engagement—especially among Millennial bible readers, who are most likely to report using digital versions of the bible.

Among those who reported reading the bible more last year, one in four said that increase happened because they were able to read on their phone or tablet. Still, most prefer to turn actual pages when they read their bible (81%), even Millennials (78%)."[1]

Personally I went digital a long time ago because it's lighter when I travel and much faster for doing research. But I do still enjoy getting out my big old leather bound bible – that's falling apart! There's still something nice about that.

❖

CHAPTER 28

Tolerance the god of this Age sits on the Throne of Culture

A dangerous new breed of Christians are arising, who are no longer willing to bow down to the culture but make a stand for their faith without apology.

"Millennials grew up in a culture where they didn't learn about religious life through cultural osmosis."

- Michael Wear

Here I want to take excerpts from author and writer Chris Martin's superb article "Millennials and the End of Osmosis Christianity," in which he writes:

"Older Millennials (born 1980-1989) grew up and younger Millennials (1990-2000) are growing up in a culture identified more by relative morality than by religious morality. But that's not the whole story.

In the early-to-mid 20th century, American culture was shaped by the God of the bible and saturated with biblical morality. My parents, and even more *their parents,* grew up in a culture in which Christianity was, consumed in a form of 'cultural osmosis.'

The Millennial Generation lives in no such culture. Today's… culture is shaped by a different god and saturated with different moral paradigms. **Tolerance is the god of this age and its moral paradigm is rooted in the freedom to pursue one's personal fulfilment at all costs.**

'Less people are calling themselves Christians and those who are will take it more seriously. In other words, cultural and congregational Christians, or the 'squishy middle,' is collapsing while convictional Christians are staying relatively steady.'

- Ed Stetzer

On the surface, it appears as though the church is bleeding members — the number of Christians in America is dwindling. But, as Stetzer observes, **what the church is losing in number, it is gaining in strength."**

So, this is somewhat encouraging, but then he goes on to speak of potential persecution, "Any matter of religion, Christian or otherwise, has become somewhat inflammatory in nature. **The god of tolerance and its relative morality has usurped the God of the bible on the throne of culture,** and tolerance has no preference for other gods or ethical systems.

Tolerance declares… 'This culture ain't big enough for the both of us.'

Misunderstanding the Gospel

When Christianity and its influence are absent from culture, society suffers. A culture void of the unconditional, sacrificial love found in the gospel of Jesus is a dark place.

Perhaps the greatest negative when it comes to the secularization of culture is that the Christian's understanding of the sinfulness of man has unnecessarily been received as **hateful bigotry.** God's Word warns us, however, of how His message is going to be received.

1 Corinthians 1:18 says, 'For the message of the cross is foolishness to those who are perishing, but it is God's power to us who are being saved.'

The things of God are foolish to those who are not of God. We cannot expect any different. The very idea a gospel that claims to be a message of 'love' would condemn certain lifestyles is absurd in the eyes of the world. When the world and everything in it is about humanity, the Word of God is foolishness.

But the world and everything in it is not about humanity and its freedom, it's about God and His glory. **When one views the gospel through the lens of eternity, it comes into focus."**[1]

I will end this book the same way that I started it, with this scripture: "For the Lord is good; his mercy is everlasting;

and his truth endureth **to all generations**" (Psalm 100:5 KJVS). "All generations," means just that. In other words, no generation is excluded or insignificant to God.

I believe that we live in the most exciting time in history. We are going to witness a breed of Christians arising (of all ages) that the world has never seen. With the resources, tools and opportunities that believers have never had. And the message is going to go forth with such power and speed, like never before. "He sendeth forth his commandment upon earth: **his word runneth very swiftly**" (Psalm 147:15 KJVS).

We can talk all day long about each and every generation and how to define them. But God has the last word. He is so much bigger than all of our thinking on this subject. He is bigger than our humanistic reasoning's, our behavioral science and even our technology. Nothing and no one can stop the power of His incorruptible Word from penetrating every single generation, one after another.

The standard for every generation is *Jesus*. He is the ultimate plumb-line that keeps us looking straight ahead. No generation can survive without Jesus at the wheel. We must surrender each and every generation to Him - our children and our children's children.

And no matter what generation we belong to, God has not finished with us yet. Every generation is relevant in His eyes and still has a contribution to make.

❖

Endnotes

Chapter 1 Understanding the Millennials

1. "It's True Millennials are Noncommittal" – by Kirsten Mikesell, TheOdysseyOnline.com, 2015.

Chapter 2 Generation Y (Millennials)

1. "Generation Y doesn't exist according to a Rouen Business School Researcher" – by Natalie Kettner (The study was published in "Revue Internationale de Psychoscoiologie") Prof. Jean Pralong 2016 also ZDNet, RHevista RH, 2010.

Chapter 4 Millennial Myopia is a Trap

1. "Millennial Myopia: A Big Social Media Trap" - by Bruce Milne, ThinkAdvisor.com, January 2015.

Chapter 5 Your Time Runs out with Logan's Run

1. Word Definition - Dystopic – a dystopia (from the Greek δυσ- and τόπος, alternatively, cacotopia, kakotopia, or simply anti-utopia) is a community or society that is undesirable or frightening. It is translated as 'not-good place,' an antonym of utopia. Wikipedia, 2017.

   An imaginary place or state in which the condition of life is extremely bad, as from deprivation, oppression, or terror. TheFreeDictionary.com, 2017.

2. Logan's Run - William F. Nolan and George Clayton Johnson, 1967 (adapted into film 1976) Wikipedia, 2017.

Chapter 7 The Generation Gap Defined

1. Work and Family Researchers Network – "Generation Gap Definition(s)" – by Robert L. Barker, p.176, 2003.

2. Definition - Generation Gap - YourDictionary.com, 2017.

3. "Generation X, Generations Y, Generation Z, and The Baby Boomers" – by Natalie Waterworth, TalentedHeads.com, 2013.

4. "Here is When Each Generation Begins and Ends According to Facts" – by Philip Bump, The Atlantic, USA, 2014.

Chapter 9 Intellectual Intolerance is on the Rise

1. "Steve Jobs was a Jerk You Shouldn't Be" – by Contributor David Coursey, Forbes.com, 2011.

2. "7 More Leadership Lessons from Steve Jobs" – by The Motley Fool Staff, Australia, 2012.

3. "Steve Jobs'… Dishonourable Behaviour" – by Peter Elkind, Fortune.com, 2015.

4. "Suffering Fools Gladly" – by David Brooks, New York Time's, Opinion Pages, 2013.

Chapter 10 Defining a Generation

1. "Millennials overtake Baby Boomers as America's Largest Generation" – by Richard Fry, Pew Research Centre, Fact Tank, News in Numbers, 2016.

2. "Millennial Definition" – UrbanDictionary.com, 2016.

Chapter 11 European Millennials

1. "Two Thirds of Italian Millennials live with their Parents" – The Local, Italy, 2016.

2. "Home Invasion" – by Hilary Osborne, The Guardian, UK, October 23, 2015.

3. "Boomerang Generation" – Wikipedia, 2017.

4. "5 Reasons God Will Not Abandon America Now" – by Rick Warren, Charisma News, 2016.

Chapter 12 Gatekeepers in the Information and Digital Age

1. Definition - "Information Age" – Wikipedia, 2016.

2. "IT Definition" – TechTerms, Sharpened Productions, 2017.

Chapter 13 Waging Lawfare

1. Definition - "Lawfare" - Wikipedia, 2017.

2. Definition - "Citizen Journalism" - Wikipedia, 2017.

3. Article - "Bill Maher on UC Berkeley's Ann Coulter Drama: This is the Liberal Version of Book Burning," by Matt Vespa, Townhall. com, April 23, 2017.

Chapter 14 What comes first the Chicken or the Egg?

1. "10 Surprising Stats and Facts about the Digital Age" – by Erik Qualman, Ragan's PR Daily, 2012.

2. "Millennials are Prioritizing Experiences Over Stuff" – by Uptin Saiidi, CNBC.com, May 5, 2016.

Chapter 15 Young Digital Shadows and Fatal Preoccupation

1. "Spain Train Crash" – by Kevin Short, Huffington Post, 2013.

2. "Top 10 Worst Cell Phone-Related Injury Accidents of All Time: Prison Edition" - Facebook updates lead to Fatal Chicago Pedestrian Accident – seriousaccidents.com - © Copyright 1998-2017, Law Offices of Michael Pines, APC. All rights reserved. San Diego, CA 92122.

Chapter 16 The War between Religion and Science

1. "Debunking the Galileo Myth" – by Dinesh D'Souza, Catholic Education Resource Center, CERC, 2007.

2. "The truth about Galileo and his conflict with the Catholic Church" – by Jessica Wolf and Professor Henry Kelly, University of California, Los Angeles, UCLA Newsroom, 2016.

3. "How Did Israel Become a Hub for Innovation?" – by Tzahi Weisfeld, Creator Wework.com, 2015.

Chapter 17 Generation X

1. "Generation X: Once Xtreme, Now Exhausted (Part 5 of 7)" – by Neil Howe, Forbes.com, 2014.

2. "Millennials overtake Baby Boomers as America's Largest Generation" – by Richard Fry, Pew Research Centre, April 25, 2016.

3. "Are You There, God? It's Me Generation X" (Who Is Generation X?) – by Jennifer McCollum, 2016.

Chapter 18 The Landmark Decision of Roe v. Wade

1. "Roe-v-Wade" - by The Editors of Encyclopædia Britannica, Britannica.com, 2017.

2. "Norma McCorvey, Jane Roe of Roe v. Wade, Dies at 69"- CBN News, The Christian Perspective, cbnnews.com, US, 2017.

Chapter 19 Gen Z Takeover

1. "The 19-year-old who's Managing Millions" (Gen Z Patrick Finnegan) – by Jackie Wattles, CNNMoney (New York) / CNN Tec, 2016.

2. "What Comes After Gen Z?" – by Laura Vanderkam and Robin Koval, Fortune Leadership, fortune.com, 2015.

Chapter 20 So Make Way for Generation Z

1. "Make Way for Generation Z" – by Alexandra Levit, New York Times, 2015.

2. "Improving Emotional Intelligence" - by Jeanne Segal, Ph.D., Melinda Smith, M.A., and Jennifer Shubin, HelpGuide.org, Emotional Health, October 2016.

Chapter 21 Gen Z – Millennials on Steroids!

1. "Millennials on Steroids" (Gen Z The Next Generation) – by Jeffrey Hayzlett, SalesForce Blog, 2016.

Chapter 22 Influencers, Disrupters and the Mavericks

1. "What comes after Generation Z?" – by Laura Vanderkam and Alexandra Levit, Fortune Leadership, fortune.com, August 10, 2015.

2. Excerpt from, "Courage to do Nothing" – by Bill Flax, ebook, Kindle Edition, September 2010.

Chapter 23 Its True Meaning – The Separation of Church and State

1. "The True Meaning of Separation of Church and State" – by Contributor Bill Flax, Forbes.com, 2011.

Chapter 24 Modern Populism v. The Babylonian System

1. "Merkel Admits Open Door Migrant Policy Mistake" – by Liam Deacon, Breitbart (breitbart.com), London UK, 2016.

2. "Palestinian Authority Pays Terrorists and Their Families $140 Million a Year" (Palestinians using foreign aid to reward terrorists for acts that kill Israelis) – by Morgan Chalfant, The Washington Free Beacon, National Security (freebeacon.com), July 7, 2016.

Chapter 25 The Rise of the Modern Populist "Movements"

1. Definition - "Five Star Movement" – Wikipedia, 2016.

2. "Ukip isn't Left wing or Right wing it's just Sensible" - by Steven Woolfe MEP, Telegraph News, Politics Blog, 2016.

Chapter 26 The Rise of the Modern Populist "Movements" Part 2

1. Definition - Populism – Business Dictionary, (businessdictionary.com), 2016.

Chapter 27 What is Globalization?

1. "What the Latest Bible Research Reveals about Millennials" – by Sarah Eekhoff Zylstra, Christianity Today, 2016.

Chapter 28 Tolerance the god of this Age sits on the Throne of Culture

1. "Millennials & the End of Osmosis Christianity" - by Chris Martin, LifeWay, Facts&Trends, factsandtrends.net, July 30, 2014, Copyright 2017.

Bibleranslations

❖

Ministry Profile

Apostle Doctor Jennifer Pateman's passion is to see the Body of Christ equipped and walking in spiritually maturity, through a married dependency on God's Spirit and Word. Her teaching ministry has a distinct prophetic flavour and she desires to see people of all ages succeed in their God given lanes.

Officially Jennifer is the Vice President of Alan Pateman Ministries (APMI) and Co-Founder of Connecting for Excellence (CFE) and LifeStyle International Christian University (LICU). She is a five-fold teaching gift to the Body of Christ, author, musician, public speaker, lecturer and researcher. Apart from travelling internationally alongside her husband, she is also acting Editorial Consultant for all LICU materials and Professor of Theology and Biblical Studies.

Most importantly Dr Jennifer is devoted to her Man of God and three beautiful children; they reside in Florence, Italy and travel out from their Apostolic Company.

- Jennifer Pateman D.Min., D.D., M.A., B.Th.

❖

To Contact the Author

Please email:

Alan Pateman Ministries International

Email: drjennifer@alanpatemanministries.com
Web: www.AlanPatemanMinistries.com

*Please include your prayer requests
and comments when you write.*

❖

Other Books by
Dr. Jennifer Pateman

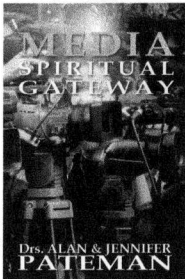

Media, Spiritual Gateway
(co-authored with Alan Pateman)

Let's face it; we live in the era of fake news! It's always existed, but never been quite so prominent. Today it's an all-out-war between fact and political fiction.

ISBN: 978-1-909132-54-2, Pages: 192,
Format: Paperback, Published: 2018
Also available in eBook format!

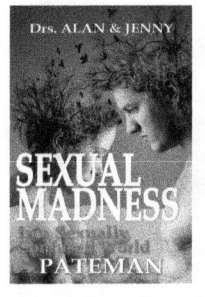

Sexual Madness, In a Sexually Confused World
(co-authored with Alan Pateman)

This book discusses the sensitive subject of political correctness in our world today and the growing fear of causing offence in the public arena. It also discusses the rise of homosexuality, pedophilia and all other forms of sexuality, as there are many. Including modern statistics on pornography.

ISBN: 978-1-909132-02-3, Pages: 160,
Format: Paperback, Published: 2012
Also available in eBook format!

Books by Apostle Dr. Alan Pateman

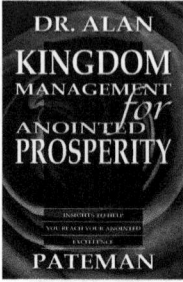

Kingdom Management for Anointed Prosperity

In his book, "Kingdom Management for Anointed Prosperity," Dr. Alan Pateman reveals how we can avoid living in continual crisis due to mismanagement. Life happens to all of us, but how we handle it matters most.

ISBN: 978-1-909132-34-4, Pages: 144, Format: Paperback, Published: 2015
Also available in eBook format!

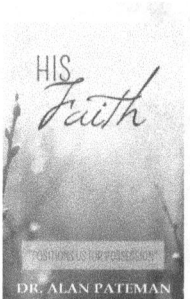

Seduction & Control: Infiltrating Society & the Church

This book is a glance into the world of seduction and control, how they try to influence the Church through many powerful avenues such as the New Age, sexual education in our schools, basic entertainment; things that touch our everyday lives in order that we effectively and gradually become desensitised.

ISBN: 978-1-909132-00-9, Pages: 156
Format: Paperback, Published: 2015
Also available in eBook format!

His Faith Positions us for Possession

It is with both simplicity and seasoned proficiency that Dr. Pateman draws us into this weighty conclusion; …only as we yield and surrender to Christ's faith IN us – will we truly be empowered to live as Christ lived on this earth, "…as he is, so are we in this world" *(1 John 4:17).*

ISBN: 978-0-9570654-0-6, Pages: 128, Format: Paperback, Published: 2014
Also available in eBook format!

Truth for the Journey Books

Forgiveness, The Key to Revival

Scripture is absolute when it comes to forgiveness. IF we forgive, THEN we are forgiven. It's that simple but no one said it was easy! Nonetheless, forgiveness can be likened to a spiritual key that unlocks spiritual doors and opportunities!

ISBN: 978-1-909132-41-2, Pages: 124,
Format: Paperback, Published: 2013
Also available in eBook format!

Why War: A Biblical Approach to the Armour of God and Spiritual Warfare

Spiritual warfare means different things to different people, but from a biblical standpoint Ephesians 6:10-18 gives us the best biblical definition of spiritual warfare possible. We can also see how God has thoroughly equipped us for victory not just self defence!

ISBN: 978-1-909132-39-9, Pages: 180,
Format: Paperback, Published: 2013
Also available in eBook format!

Revival Fires - Anointed Generals Past & Present (Part Two of Four)

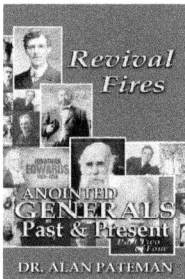

Seasons might be changing but God's Word remains the same. The heart of the author is to help train, equip and be a blessing to those men and women who will be willing to fulfil their potential in ministry and be properly equipped for service.

ISBN: 978-1-909132-36-8, Pages: 142,
Format: Paperback, Published: 2012
Also available in eBook format!

Truth for the Journey Books

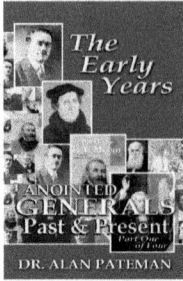

The Early Years - Anointed Generals
Past & Present (Part One of Four)

I pray that the divine anointing that is and has been upon these *Anointed Generals Past and Present* will be afforded to flow upon our heads, that those who are reported to be the generals of today would be strong enough - humble enough - to give time to those who desire to learn and grow and be established. So that what God has given to them will be our inheritance for the future.

ISBN: 978-1-909132-32-0, Pages: 132,
Format: Paperback, Published: 2012
Also available in eBook format!

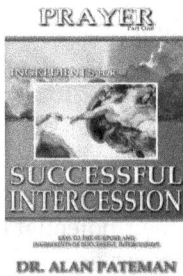

Prayer, Touching the Heart of God (Part Two)

Touching the Heart of God is the very essence of prayer. Whether we are petitioning God with very specific requests or consecrating ourselves before Him and rededicating our lives - whatever the case may be – the true essence of all praying is "Touching the Heart of God."

ISBN: 978-1-909132-12-2, Pages: 180,
Format: Paperback, Published: 2012
Also available in eBook format!

Prayer, Ingredients for Successful Intercession
(Part One)

This Book is the first of two books on Prayer. Dr. Pateman provides an exhaustive study, showcasing the vital ingredients necessary for all successful prayer. An excellent power-packed teaching tool, either for the individual or for the local church prayer group, that's eager to lay a solid foundation but don't know where to start!

ISBN: 978-1-909132-11-5, Pages: 140,
Format: Paperback, Published: 2012
Also available in eBook format!

Apostles: Can the Church Survive Without Them?

Before Jesus returns a significant increase of the anointing will be poured out on the Body of Christ, but can the Church handle such an anointing? *(Acts 5:5)* Billy Brim once said, "As much as the anointing is powerful to create, it is as powerfully destructive of evil." The fear of God will be restored with the apostolic and people will begin walking with such anointing, as we have never seen before!

ISBN: 978-1-909132-04-7, Pages: 164,
Format: Paperback, Published: 2012
Also available in eBook format!

TONGUES, Our Supernatural Prayer Language

In writing to the church at Corinth, Paul encouraged them to continue the practice of speaking with other tongues in their worship of God and in their prayer lives as a means of spiritual edification.

ISBN: 978-1-909132-44-3, Pages: 144,
Format: Paperback, Published: 2016
Also available in eBook format!

His Life is in the Blood

Blood is the trophy of every battle. The spilt blood of Jesus Christ is our trophy. It is our freedom from sin and bondage. Nothing can enter the blood-bought temples of the Holy Ghost! This book will encourage you to apply the blood of Jesus our Passover Lamb to your life, just as the children of Israel did in the Old Testament. Not merely talking or reading about it, but applying it.

ISBN: 978-1-909132-06-1, Pages: 152,
Format: Paperback, First Published: 2007
Also available in eBook format!

Dear Friends,

Have you considered becoming one of our international students? We are privileged to welcome you, from around the world, to "LifeStyle International Christian University" *(the teaching arm of Alan Pateman Ministries International).* **An English speaking university** dedicated to your success; to see you trained and equipped to fully succeed in your God given Destiny.

It is our passion to raise up the leaders of tomorrow, who will have influence in all realms of authority, including the Body of Christ. Men and women of strategy, wisdom and true godliness, who'll stand with stature and maturity in this hour.

It's undeniable that in today's world, recognised education has become indispensable, therefore it is our desire to offer well balanced and well structured courses. Those that have been written by gifted and talented ministers of God, who seek to be inspired by God's Holy Spirit.

Consequently we have put together a **flexible curriculum,** designed both for correspondence students and campuses, which is a strategy to reach the distant learner; whether provincial, national or international. In fact we have many correspondence students from around the world, including a growing number of successful campuses, in various countries.

This is a growing platform, where men and women of dignity and passion, can grow and be established in their God given endeavours. As God is the healer of the nations, we pray and believe that many of our alumni will go on to **become world changers** in their own right.

We are proud of each and every one of our LICU students.
It would be our pleasure if you would join them on this incredible journey!

Doctor Alan Pateman

Alan Pateman Prof. Ph.D., D.Min., D.D., M.A., B.Th.
PRESIDENT AND CEO
www.licuuniversity.com www.cfeapostolicnetwork.com
Email: info@licuuniversity.com   Mob: +39 366 329 1315

For more information visit our website/facebook or contact our office, using the details below:

Website: www.licuuniversity.com
Facebook: www.facebook.com/LICUMainCampus
Email: info@licuuniversity.com
Telephone: +39 366 329 1315

All Books Available

at

APMI PUBLICATIONS

Email: publications@alanpateman.com
Also Available from Amazon.com
and other retail outlets.

If you purchased this book through Amazon.com or other and enjoyed reading it, or perhaps one of my other books, I would be grateful if you could take a couple of minutes to write a Customer Review, many thanks.